PREVENTIVE MAINTENANCE FOR HIGHER EDUCATION FACILITIES

Applied Management Engineering, Inc.

RSMeans

WILEY

John Wiley & Sons, Inc.

PREVENTIVE MAINTENANCE

FOR HIGHER EDUCATION FACILITIES

A Planning & Budgeting Tool for Facilities Professionals

- *Establishing the Value of PM*
- *Defining the Requirements*
- *Quantifying the Cost*
- *Prioritizing Within Budget Constraints*

Applied Management Engineering, Inc.

The editors for this book were Phil Waier, Steve Plotner, and Andrea St. Ours. The managing editor was Mary Greene. The production manager was Michael Kokernak. The production coordinator was Marion Schofield. The electronic publishing specialist was Paula Reale-Camelio. The proofreader was Robin Richardson. The book and cover were designed by Norman R. Forgit.

For general information on our other products and services, or technical support, please contact our Customer Care Department within the United States at 800-762-2974, outside the United States at 317-572-3993 or fax 317-572-4002.

Wiley also publishes its books in a variety of electronic formats. Some content that appears in print may not be available in electronic books. For more information about Wiley products, visit our web site at www.wiley.com.

Library of Congress Cataloging-in-Publication Data:

ISBN: 978-1-118-16671-0

Printed in the United States of America

10 9 8 7 6 5 4

TABLE OF CONTENTS

Appendix/Index

FOREWORD

For today's institutional facilities manager, preventive maintenance offers a great opportunity, but also a challenge. The very feature that makes PM cost effective is the same feature that makes it the first to be cut. PM is a *planned* activity. Unfortunately because there is a plan, the organization can just plan to *not* make it part of their maintenance operation.

All too often an assumption is made that purchasing a computerized maintenance management system (CMMS) will fulfill the requirement for a PM program. This is analogous to the idea that a new accounting system will save a failing business. While it's true that a failing business will need an accounting system to organize the firms financial transactions, the business will only be successful when management uses the information available to make the best business decisions, or at least minimize the poor ones. A CMMS system will not solve the PM problem; it will only assist in management's implementation of the correct decisions to successfully run the required level of PM.

This book is designed to help the facilities manager increase the life of facility systems and equipment, lower overall operating costs, and provide maximum responsiveness to the college/ university community. One obstacle to these goals is equipment deterioration. The rate of deterioration and failure is the result of several factors: poor installation, wrong application, adverse environmental conditions, human errors (on the part of operators and maintenance personnel), normal wear and tear, and insufficient maintenance.

Operating to failure costs significantly more than failure avoidance and planned repairs and replacements through PM. It is particularly expensive when an unexpected failure endangers personnel; releases toxic, flammable, or polluting material; interrupts operations; or causes collateral damage. Unexpected failures generally cause outages and may inflict damage well beyond the affected component. If inspected routinely, however, most equipment provides some warning of impending failure, such as vibration energy, noise, and heat (or lack of heat).

Part One of this book is designed to address the institutional facility manager's preventive maintenance challenges and to provide the necessary information to determine the appropriate direction. The tools in Part Two—models of typical campus buildings—will help to answer the question, "What resources are required to implement a PM program if I could fully fund it?" Then, assuming that the budget does not allow for full funding, as is sometimes the case, it addresses what the optimal way is to allocate PM resources to achieve a successful PM program.

Parts Two and Three of this book include data based on the preventive maintenance section of R.S. Means' *Facilities Maintenance & Repair Cost Data*. This annually updated publication, first released in 1993, represented a milestone in the industry in that it provided PM tasks, frequencies, and cost data for much of the plant equipment found in higher education institutions. This book, like the PM section of *Facilities Maintenance & Repair Cost Data*, gives you practical information on PM requirements that is not available from other sources.

Some might ask why a facility manager would not use manufacturers' guides as a source of required PM tasks. Here are a few key reasons:

- Manufacturers' guides are extensive, and are created for the primary purpose of protecting the manufacturer during the warranty period, rather than for the entire life cycle of the equipment.

- Using manufacturers' guides forever would be too costly because the impact of operation and on-going maintenance is not considered.

- True PM requirements should be based on actual usage, location, design, installation, and overall maintenance history.

This book is designed with the higher education community in mind. Each college/university facility will have a primary usage, such as a dormitory, classroom, gymnasium, and so forth. New preventive maintenance checklists were developed for this book to reflect the mission criticality of these facility types. The college/university equipment, and the classification of each building, is the fundamental basis of this book. Additionally, the book is unique in that a dedicated Website is provided to enable the user to modify their particular facility/equipment considerations, and receive immediate results. The address is:

http://www.rsmeans.com/supplement/pmhighed.html

ACKNOWLEDGMENTS

AME appreciates the efforts of the following individuals at R.S. Means Company, Inc. who provided technical and editorial review and suggestions for this publication: Phil Waier, Principal Engineer; Steve Plotner, Senior Engineer/Editor; Mary Greene, Managing Editor; and Andrea Keenan, Manuscript Editor. We are also grateful to Eric Dillinger of Carter & Burgess, Inc. in Fort Worth, Texas for serving as reviewer of this publication, and to Jim Armstrong of Shooshanian Engineering in Boston, MA for his input during the book's conceptual development.

ABOUT THE AUTHORS

Applied Management Engineering, Inc. (AME), located in Virginia Beach, Virginia, provides facility engineering and management consulting services to both public and private sector organizations. Established in 1980, the company has set industry standards for facility management consulting in the following areas:

- Condition Assessments
- Facility Management Consulting
- Maintenance and Repair Cost Estimating
- Preventive and Predictive Maintenance Programs
- Facilities Management Training
- Re-Engineering and Rightsourcing Analysis
- Maintenance Management Software Development and Evaluation

AME continues to expand its resources and capabilities in all fields of facility engineering and management consulting. Among AME's clients are federal, state, and municipal entities, as well as numerous college and university facilities throughout the U.S., including:

- Duke University
- Northwestern University
- Brown University
- University of Rochester

- University of Vermont
- University of California at San Diego, Berkeley
- Ohio University
- San Jacinto College
- Virginia Community College System

AME can be reached at 1-800-532-0763 or by e-mail at ame@ameinc.biz. The company Website is: **http://www.ameinc.biz**

Other publications that AME has authored include the following.

- *Developing & Managing Condition Assessment Programs,* R.S. Means, Company, Inc.
- *Means Facilities Maintenance & Repair Cost Data* (PM Section), R.S. Means Company, Inc.
- *Maintenance Management Audit,* R.S. Means Company, Inc.
- *Managing the Facilities Portfolio,* National Association of College and University Business Officers

Part One

PM IN HIGHER EDUCATION FACILITIES: SELLING THE NEED

PM IN HIGHER EDUCATION FACILITIES

Introduction   Preventive maintenance (PM) can be defined as periodic, scheduled work on selected equipment, usually consisting of required inspection, lubrication, and minor adjustment. PM has been generally accepted as a cost-effective approach to good maintenance practice within the facilities management community. It extends equipment life, reduces the number of service calls, and limits the potential collateral damage to facility systems, personnel, and mission from equipment failures. It is important to note that PM does not include time for repairs or replacement of major parts. Any additional work required should be identified during the PM inspection and accomplished later as a separate work order.

If PM is accepted as cost-effective, then why is it seldom completely implemented in the college and university environment? The reason is that facility managers often have difficulty selling the benefits to their institutional customers and governing boards, as well as quantifying the annual cost of implementing a PM program. The long-term cost benefits and avoidance of collateral damage are often difficult, if not impossible, to quantify. Since there is no immediate feedback or gratification from PM as there is with aesthetic improvements such as painting and carpeting, the customer cannot readily appreciate its impact. However, a crisis resulting from the lack of PM, such as equipment failure, always receives immediate attention.

Facility mangers often try to sell the need for a program without being able to answer the three most important questions:

1. What will it *cost* annually to implement a PM program?

2. What is the *impact* if a PM program is not implemented?

3. What is *required* to fully implement a PM program?

To address the requirements of a PM program, this book describes the steps to implement a complete program and provides facility managers with a cost-effective method to "make the sale" and develop a plan for implementation. (This includes the use of a Computerized Maintenance Management System [CMMS] when applicable. Refer to the Appendix for more information on CMMS implementation.)

What is the Annual Cost of PM?

To answer the first question, this book provides models for thirteen functional building types found in higher education facilities, which identify the systems and equipment types to be included in the PM program. Factors considered for inclusion were the criticality of the system and/or piece of equipment, impact on other systems and equipment, and the economic justification for the expense of performing PM. To help determine the annual cost of a PM program, facility managers can review the models and select the one that most resembles each of their actual facilities. They can then apply the model data to their own facilities, based on square footage costs.

The models also provide detailed equipment quantities, PM standards and labor-hours, and recommended frequencies for each of four priority levels. This enables the user to refine the models to more accurately reflect their portfolio of facilities. *(For more on the specific building models and how to use them, see Part Two of this book.)*

Addressing the impact if a PM program is not implemented is more complicated. Quantifying cost-avoidance and economic payback on extended life of equipment is difficult due to the lack of back-up data. Accurately tracking costs for a system or piece of equipment over a life cycle of 4–20 years is more probable with today's computerized management systems. However, a 20-year body of data does not currently exist for analysis. The expected return on investment by implementing a preventive maintenance program is therefore more *implied* than actually measured on a true economic analysis basis.

When considering whether or not to commit to a service or program, most institutional managers will want to analyze the cost benefits. This publication provides a logical approach to address this issue in lieu of many years of accumulated hard data. The Appendix of this book provides PM return on investments (ROI) examples that provide cash-flow scenarios relating short-term resources with long-term results.

Material Costs

Material typically consumed in the PM process includes belts, grease, oil, rags, and miscellaneous hardware. The cost of these materials is minor and is usually included in shop or plant overhead. For the approach provided in this book, material requirements are considered as minimal expenses included in the hourly rates, and do not provide an impact on the square foot costs of the models. However, users may consider including actual material expenses based on their individual location, equipment requirements, and local area statutory requirements.

Recent indoor air quality concerns have additionally had a direct effect of the complexity of air filters and their replacement cycles. Filter types may include roll, disposable, pleated surface, extended pleated surface, box, and HEPA. Costs can range from $1 to nearly $200 each. For example, a 25-ton air-handling unit might require 30 to 40 filters per year to maintain proper environmental conditions.

Loss of Equipment Life

What Is the Impact If PM Is Not Implemented?

Equipment life cycle is a difficult issue to monitor. The management truism, "If you can't measure it, you can't manage it," describes the problem quite well. While PM typically maximizes equipment life, reduces the number of service calls, and limits collateral damage to the facility, when it comes to quantifying the extension of equipment life, its benefits are more difficult to measure.

It is difficult to quantify the life-cycle cost-avoidance associated with a PM program without detailed historical costs. Many university buildings are more than 100 years old, and their equipment repair and replacement have been handled by a combination of in-house and contracted services. While the current trend of tracking assets with CMMS programs should result in more accurate data for future analysis, historical equipment records are seldom available beyond a 3–5 year period.

Equipment will fail based on several factors, including poor design, installation, usage, maintenance, environment, and abuse. *Breakdown maintenance,* or *run-to-failure,* pays little attention to ensuring that equipment reaches the end of its expected life. This approach allows equipment to operate until it can no longer perform its intended function or it catastrophically fails. The extent of the damage resulting from unplanned breakdown maintenance is typically greater than if PM were performed, because the problem was not identified until equipment completely failed.

When considering implementing a PM program, the issue of return on investment will inevitably be raised. To illustrate a simplified approach in response, a sample format of a life-cycle cash flow analysis can be found in the Appendix of this book. This format provides a straightforward method to discuss equipment ROI/payback. Use of this format requires several assumptions that point to the challenge of determining the return on investment. For example, the impact of catastrophic failure (and its associated dollar value) must be projected. Factors such as building usage, location, and equipment operation must also be approximated. A rigorous life-cycle analysis would require hard data to back up these assumptions, and the effort of collecting it may exceed the benefit of the desired result.

Increase of Service Calls

The direct consequence of not conducting PM is generally reflected by an increase in the number of service or trouble calls. While the customer may think a service call is the fastest way to get a request processed, a successful PM program should prevent the need for the customer to make a request in the first place.

Service calls tend to be expensive and an inefficient way to manage facilities. The response to a call for assistance typically involves wasted trips or multiple trips to the work site, for a variety of reasons including:

- False Alarm: No problem to fix.
- Work Content: Work involved not clearly defined by caller (wrong trade, for example).
- Inconvenient: The task must be done at another time.
- Tools/Parts: Additional tools, equipment, or help are needed.
- Previously Done: Some other entity has already fixed the problem.
- Out of Scope: The task is too large to address as a service call.
- Other situations such as responsibility, payment, etc.

In each of the above instances, time is expended, typically by a crew of two, but no maintenance need is met. The "lost" charges due to the cost of inefficient service calls may be captured as overhead charges, or charged to other open or standing job orders. Facility management organizations tend to not properly capture these inefficiencies for documentation and analysis.

The difference between the distribution of labor and material costs for service call work versus planned work orders is typically significant, further emphasizing the benefits of a fully-implemented PM program. A large group of well-planned maintenance work orders tends to average a labor/material distribution of 60% labor and 40% material, while a group of service calls will be approximately 90% labor and 10% material. A planned work order will require fewer labor-hours than a service call of similar work content. In fact, labor requirements may actually be multiplied several times when work is done as a service call. The following example shows the potential differences.

Example

A series of service call-type work orders that costs $10,000 to accomplish may be distributed at:

$9,000.00 Labor (90%)
+ $1,000.00 Material (10%)
= $10,000.00 Total Cost

Well-planned work requirements that have the same overall material requirements:

$1,500.00 Labor (60%)
+ $1,000.00 Material (40%)
= $2,500.00 Total Cost

Thus, work done as a series of service calls costs the university four times what it should cost. Again, the goal is to minimize, to the extent practical, the dependence on service calls.

Potential Collateral Damage

During the life cycle of equipment, unanticipated breakdowns will occur. The facility manager must estimate the loss resulting from both direct and collateral damages.

Direct damage includes expenses associated with repairing the equipment as an emergency. The magnitude of direct damages for equipment, without PM performed, would be expected to be higher because the damage was not identified until the equipment failed, rather than during a planned shutdown for repair. This type of failure often results in collateral damage to associated equipment components.

Collateral damage is typically associated with unscheduled equipment failure. Costs can be significant and difficult to approximate. Some of the damage may not be directly associated with a one-time repair cost, but may have intangible impact, such as the loss of prestige. The following list represents factors that might add to collateral damage expenses.

- Relocating students, staff, projects, delicate materials, or critical equipment until the condition has been corrected.

- Unexpected expenses for renting and installing temporary replacement equipment to keep the facility operational, delicate materials from damage, or critical equipment operating.

- Consultant services associated with repairing or replacing the failed equipment.

- Liabilities incurred from outsiders or employees from personal injuries or property damage resulting from failed equipment or systems.

- Loss of prestige or reputation resulting from failed equipment or systems, particularly if the failure coincides with an important event.

What Is Required to Fully Implement a PM Program?

After determining the resource requirements for a PM program by using the PM models in this book and adequately describing the impact of *not* implementing a PM program, the next step is to prepare a milestone plan to fully implement the program.

Inventory

The backbone of a PM program is the equipment inventory. Once the decision has been made as to the types of equipment to be included in the PM program, the development of an equipment inventory can proceed.

The inventory requires a survey of systems and equipment data. This data should include the facility name and number, equipment location within the facility, system/equipment identifier, equipment description, priority, manufacturer and model number, size/capacity, volts, amperes, and associated systems that could be affected. Applicable PM Standards/Checklists should also be documented. The inventory should include special information that would aid in performing PM, such as the number of belts or filters and their sizes.

PM Standards/Checklists

In order to plan and schedule a PM program, and ensure that it is accomplished, it is necessary to define the PM tasks (checkpoints) and frequencies applicable to each piece of equipment included in the PM program. This information is referred to as *PM Standards/ Checklists* in this book.

Identical pieces of equipment installed in buildings with different operating requirements or functions may require different PM tasks and different frequencies. The PM Standards/Checklists provided in Part Three can serve as guides, as they set forth the typical PM steps and labor-hours for each piece of equipment. Users can tailor or add new PM Standards/Checklists to fit special operating requirements of equipment, using the electronic versions on the book's Website. The Website address is: **http://www.rsmeans.com/ supplement/pmhighed.html** *(See Parts Two and Three for more on customizing the building models and PM Standards/Checklists.)*

Schedule

The next step in implementing a PM program is to develop a schedule. A PM Schedule assigns each PM task in the Standards/ Checklists to an appropriate inspection frequency—weekly, monthly, semi-annually, or annually. The shop labor-hour assignments are designed to distribute the labor-hour requirements evenly throughout the year. Good planning can limit the amount of travel time each day. Assigning multiple tasks in the same facility will result in a more practical use of the mechanic's time.

PM Execution

The last step is the actual implementation of the PM program. When the user first begins the program, the cumulative effect of all previous maintenance decisions will need to be addressed. The fact is that a new PM program is not going to instantly "correct" all of the problems that may have resulted from previous maintenance approaches. The facility manager will need some sort of benchmark or " snapshot" of current conditions, as well as some indication of any significant problems anticipated in the future.

To benchmark and appraise progress, a standard set of reports should be reviewed and analyzed periodically. One of the easiest ways to establish such a benchmark is to track service calls. A database could be set up to monitor the total number of calls in a given period (say a year, month, week, etc.), keeping track of them by building. The next step is to track distribution by trade, followed by what systems are affected, linking the information to each piece of equipment. This sort of analysis would begin to paint a picture of where problems are, and what systems and pieces of equipment are affected. Management can then begin to ask what is being done in terms of PM for those systems, and if the systems and equipment are even *included* in the PM program.

Appraisal

The final piece of a PM program is an appraisal of how the system is working. The appraisal, which is on-going, uses performance data to make business decisions. The result, which is management taking action to keep problems from recurring, is based on the review of completed jobs and projects, variance or exception reports, and feedback from customers.

The appraisal may reveal a need to increase or decrease the service interval for PM visits. It may also lead to adding or subtracting PM tasks for individual pieces of equipment, or actually deleting pieces of equipment from the PM program altogether. The important thing is to recognize that the PM program is a work plan that requires on going management review and refinement.

Business Process Analysis

Business Process Analysis refers to the impact a particular product or service has on an organization. While universities are not businesses in the strict sense, they do tend to strive to operate according to industry practices and have bottom-line responsibility. In effect, the question is, "Does the product or service improve the way we do business?" For the purpose of this publication, the question can be restated as, "Does the implementation of a PM program improve the reliability of services that we provide to the customer?"

One tool that can help answer this question is *Maintenance Management Audit,* published by R.S. Means Company. The book provides an analysis of how maintenance is managed and performed and uses five basic components and 37 key elements to evaluate the effectiveness of a maintenance management program.

The business process analysis should be structured to follow the actual maintenance management process, set up such that components and/or elements can be regrouped, added, or deleted to match your particular type of maintenance management organization. The five basic components, which follow the sequential steps of the major functional areas of maintenance management, are listed below.

The first component, *Organization*, includes the essential management activities that guide policies and procedures. The organizational structure is evaluated to identify lines of responsibility and supervision.

The next component, *Workload Identification*, addresses the way(s) in which needed work is documented and brought to the attention of the maintenance organization.

Under *Work Planning*, the methods used to perform work are evaluated. Prioritizing, planning, estimating, and budgeting are all tasks that control the flow of work accomplished by shop forces and contractors.

The *Work Accomplishment* component describes various support activities that enable the maintenance management organization to perform efficiently. Available personnel, materials, equipment, transportation, staff training and supervision, and contracting procedures are evaluated.

The *Appraisal* component summarizes the information needed to monitor the comparison of actual to planned results and evaluate the differences between budgeted and actual costs and performance.

The maintenance management review process evaluates the effectiveness of the existing maintenance management system by assessing each of the key elements to obtain an overview of the program's effectiveness. This overview provides:

- A program effectiveness rating
- Identification of areas for potential improvement
- A broad indication of potential productivity gains

The first step of the review process is the maintenance management effectiveness analysis, which is designed to improve productivity. Questions asked of the organization include:

- How is it organized?
- How does it function?
- How effective is its operation?

This model can be used to provide a subjective quantification of overall program effectiveness. A maintenance management system that has all components fully implemented will achieve an excellent rating. Where improvement is indicated, an action plan with specific recommendations for improving the current process should be developed. Figure 1.1 depicts the flow of work involved in an action plan. *(See the Appendix for a checklist to rate your PM program.)*

Preventive Maintenance and Facilities Condition Assessment

It is important to note that PM is generally applied to equipment that is dynamic in nature. This should not be confused with a Facility Condition Assessment (FCA) program. An FCA program can be defined as, "a planned and organized visual inspection performed by selected and trained personnel that will produce complete and quantitative reports of deficiencies, recommend maintenance priorities, and provide credible work planning and budget support data" (*Maintenance Management Audit*, an R.S. Means publication). The two programs are similar in nature in that they both consist of regular, routine, on-site inspection. However, they differ in how corrective action is identified and addressed. These differences can be broken down as follows.

Inspection

PM: Inspects immediate condition of specific components.

FCA: Inspects both immediate and long-range condition of major pieces of equipment and systems.

Corrective Action

PM: Adjusts/lubricates (corrective actions) immediately.

FCA: Recommends corrective actions to take place in a prioritized order.

The point of making this distinction is that an organization should not "PM" a building, parking lot, fence, or sidewalk. Those type of real property assets should be assessed periodically, resulting in a list of corrective actions, prioritized based on age, impact, liability, and so forth. A plan of action can then be developed over time to complete the required corrective actions.

However, the two programs should not stand separate and distinct. In essence, both a PM and FCA program should be part of an overall maintenance strategy that addresses recurring maintenance, life cycle, and work types in addition to building age, use, and other long-term considerations.

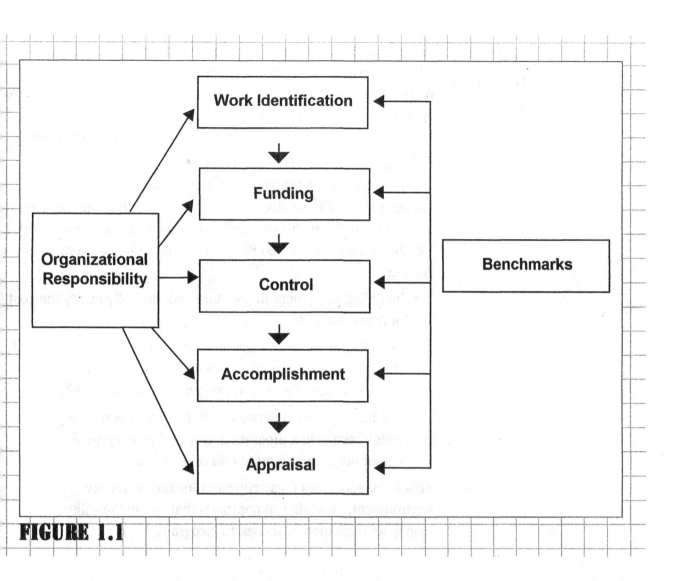

FIGURE 1.1

11

The PM Solution

Preventive maintenance has been generally accepted as a cost-effective way of extending equipment life. Implementing a PM program can prevent catastrophic failures, reduce the downtime of systems and equipment, eliminate premature replacement of equipment, and reduce the collateral damage to other equipment, personnel, and facilities.

Many university PM programs are inadequate because the facility manager has not been able to "sell" the university administration on the cost and benefits of a well-functioning PM program. Without a dedicated and structured PM plan, the program can contain flaws such as:

- Including equipment that cannot economically justify the cost of performing PM.

- Including maintenance that is inadequate for the criticality of the systems and equipment, as well as maintenance that should be classified as recurring work rather than PM.

- Not having enough personnel dedicated to performing PM, which results in a program that is performed only when personnel are not required on other projects.

This book addresses these concerns for the university environment, providing an approach that will help facility managers implement a successful program.

Part Two

CAMPUS BUILDING MODELS WITH EQUIPMENT

HOW TO USE THE BUILDING MODELS

This section provides thirteen typical campus building models to help facility managers estimate the annual labor-hours required for a PM program and easily quantify potential costs. The models were developed according to the following parameters.

- Functional building types (models) were selected that are representative of facilities found on a higher education campus.

- For most building types included two representative sizes were developed, defined by square footage and number of stories, for each building type.

- An inventory of systems and equipment was developed to be included in the PM program for each building type.

- PM Standards/Checklists were assigned to each system and piece of equipment to be included in the program. They outline the required PM tasks, labor-hours per task, and frequency assigned to each task.

Selection of Functional Building Types and Sizes

The functional building types represent the basic facilities found on today's university campus. Figure 2.1 is a list of the models included in this book. Please note that it is not intended to cover every type of facility on a campus. In general, all facilities could be included in the PM program. Utility buildings have been excluded because they normally have full-time personnel to operate, monitor, and perform maintenance on the utility equipment. For other types of buildings to be included in the PM program, a similar approach can be used and additional models developed.

Selection of Equipment, Quantities, and Frequencies

Each building model has been evaluated to identify the type, size, and quantity of systems and equipment that typically require PM. Equipment selection and PM requirements are based on the authors' condition assessment projects for numerous colleges and universities throughout the United States.

It is not practical or cost effective to perform PM on all equipment within a facility. Many times replacement components may be less expensive to ignore than to routinely service. This is often referred to as *run-to-failure*. Also, servicing numerous components can often exceed the cost of replacement. Travel time, parts storage, and access costs should be carefully considered to determine what should be included in the PM program.

It is important to note that systems or components not included in the PM program are candidates for run-to-failure repair (unplanned), programmed major maintenance (planned), or

Type	Stories	Area (SF)
Classroom #1	1-2	90,000
Classroom #2	2-4	240,000
Administration #1	1-2	60,000
Administration #2	3-6	100,000
Dormitory #1	1-3	50,000
Dormitory #2	4-8	170,000
Gymnasium #1	1	20,000
Gymnasium #2	3	120,000
Laboratory #1	1-2	45,000
Laboratory #2	3-4	100,000
Library #1	2-4	60,000
Library #2	4-5	400,000
Performing Arts Center	1-2	50,000

FIGURE 2.1 *Functional Building Types*

planned maintenance and repair based on condition and need. Typically, components included in a run-to-failure strategy are smaller, non-critical items that can be repaired or replaced on a minor work order.

In order to plan, schedule, and carry out the PM program, the PM tasks (checkpoints) and frequencies for each piece of equipment included in the program must first be defined. The PM Standards/ Checklists, in Part Three of this publication, are based on *Means Facilities Maintenance & Repair Cost Data* and are customized to higher education facilities. Identical pieces of equipment installed in buildings with different operating requirements will have different frequencies. The facility manager may also add or tailor any of the PM checklists to fit any special operating requirements of their particular facility.

The factors considered for inclusion of equipment, quantities, and frequencies are the criticality of the system and/or equipment, the impact on other systems and equipment, and the economic justification for the expense of performing PM. Each model has been carefully planned and structured to generally include only those items that meet the objectives delineated above.

How to Interpret the PM Models

The building models in this book provide the necessary information to enable the user to determine the overall labor-hours required to accomplish the identified work. They include the annual labor-hours required to perform PM on the kind of equipment one might expect to find in each functional building type. The models consist of two-page fold-outs for each of the thirteen functional building types. Below is an explanation of how to interpret the data presented in them.

Model Segments

The building models have been separated into Segments A, B, and C to help the user understand the format. A description of each model segment follows (refer to Figure 2.2). Following this is a more detailed breakdown of each component within the segments.

Segment A is a listing of the dynamic equipment inventory for the model. It contains the Checklist/System Line Number (refer to Block 1 in Figure 2.2), Equipment Types (Block 2), and Total Quantity of Each Type of Equipment (Block 3) for the building model. The selected equipment types and their quantities for each model represent the equipment that might be included in a PM program. The Checklist/System Line Number refers to the PM Standard/Checklist from *Means Facilities Maintenance & Repair Cost Data*, (FM&R), assigned to each Equipment Type.

Segment B is the application of the PM Standards/Checklists to the equipment inventories in Segment A, and utilizes the Annualized Labor-Hours of Each Type of Equipment (Block 4) and the Labor-Hours by PM Frequencies to identify the labor-hours assigned to the total quantity of each equipment type. The labor-hours identified in a frequency column across from the tasks (Block 5) are the product of the labor-hours (identified in the same frequency column of the PM Standard/Checklist) the quantity of equipment assigned to the model (Block 3). The sum of the Labor-Hours by PM Frequencies is the Total Annualized Labor-Hours for Each Equipment Type (Block 6).

The Shop Labor-Hours by PM Frequencies represents the sum of the labor-hours identified in the frequency columns sorted by trade, such as fire protection, conveying, and heating and cooling (Block 7). The Total Shop Annualized Labor-Hours in the total column, across from each shop, is the sum of all the labor-hours by frequencies, sorted by trade.

The Labor-Hour per 10,000 SF box provides the total annualized labor-hours for the model divided by the number of 10,000 SF units contained in the model (Block 8).

Segment C illustrates a potential phased approach to PM for the model based on the assumption that resources are limited. This segment provides logical levels of PM as a progressive process to stay within resource limitations. The frequency assigned to a task directly relates to the impact that the failure of a component has to the continued operation of that equipment and the mission of the facility. The greater the effect, the more frequent inspection is required of the components that could fail. Another factor considered is the economic impact of performing the tasks. All components in a piece of equipment do not require the same level of inspection in order to maintain the equipment in proper working order. Users can expect to tailor the PM program to their available resources. *(Note: See "Application Techniques" and "Customizing the Models" later in this section.)*

Model Sections

The following is a detailed explanation, section by section, of the PM models. (See Figure 2.2 for a graphic explanation.) Next to each bold number below is a description of each item, followed by a sample entry in parentheses and italics.

1 **Checklist System/Line Number** *(PM8.2-270-1950)*: Each PM standard has been assigned a unique identification number that corresponds to the UniFormat classification system and R.S. Means' own numbering system. The first number (8, for example) represents the UniFormat division. The division number paired with the next number (8.3, in this example) signifies Means' subdivision. The next three numbers following the first hyphen (270) represent Means' major classification, and the final four digits (1950) are Means' individual line number.

2 **Equipment Type** *(Fire Alarm Annunciator System)*: A one-line description of each equipment type to be included in the PM program.

3 **Total Quantity of Each Equipment Type** *(1)*: The estimated number of each equipment type that one might expect to find in the facility.

4 **Annualized Labor-Hours for Each Equipment** *(11.050)*: The number of annual labor-hours required to perform the required PM tasks on a single piece of equipment.

5 **Labor-Hours by PM Frequency for Total Quantities of Equipment** *(M = 4.472, Q = 1.118, S = 2.730, A = 2.730)*: The columns are marked with the "W" for weekly, "M" for monthly, "Q" for Quarterly, "S" for semi-annually, and "A" for annually, which indicate the recommended frequency to perform a task. The number in each frequency column, across from each equipment type, represents the total labor-hours required to carry out these tasks based on the frequencies given and the quantity of equipment found in the model. Color-coding was assigned to each frequency to help identify their assignment to the levels in Segment C. *(Note: See item number nine below for more on what each color symbolizes.)*

6 **Total Annualized Labor-Hours for Each Equipment Type** *(11.050)*: The sum of the annual labor-hours for all PM frequencies is based on the quantity of each equipment type.

7 **Labor-Hours by Shop** *(Fire Protection Shop Labor-Hours by Frequency, M = 11.600, Q = 4.432, S = 4.387, A = 7.606, and Total = 28.025)*: The columns marked with a "W" for weekly, "M" for monthly, "Q" for Quarterly, "S" for semi-annually, and "A" for annually indicate the frequency when PM is to be performed. The number in each frequency column across from each shop represents the total labor-hours for the frequencies for all the equipment assigned to that shop. The number in the total column, across from each shop, represents the sum total of all the labor-hours for the frequencies for all the equipment assigned to that shop. These numbers can be used to determine the resources required to initiate a PM program for a 90,000 square foot classroom building, for example.

8 **Labor-Hours per 10,000 SF** *(20.1)*: The labor requirements per 10,000 square feet for the particular building model. This number can be used in the estimating process to calculate the annual PM program labor-hour requirements. It can also be used to determine the resources required to initiate a PM program, based on each 10,000 square feet of a 90,000 square foot classroom building, for example.

9 **Classification of Importance in the Implementation of a PM Program** *(Level 1, 2, 3, 4)*: A classification of PM requirements to aid in estimating PM implementation costs. The levels were selected to be applied according to the available resources, criticality of the equipment, and the effect on the mission of the facility.

The levels and their assigned colors are defined as follows.

Level 1, Life-Safety Labor-Hours: Level 1 is reserved for equipment that is considered critical from a life-safety standpoint. The column includes the total annual PM labor-hour requirements for the equipment that falls into this category. A dark blue color represents all frequencies assigned to Level 1.

Level 2, Labor-Hours: Level 2 is assigned to systems and equipment that are considered mission-essential. This column includes the total annual PM labor-hour requirements for equipment that falls into this category. If resources do not allow for the application of total annual labor-hours, users may choose to apply the annual and semi-annual frequency labor-hour requirements. Additional labor-hours for the remaining frequencies can be further distributed to Level 3 and 4 categories. It is important to note that the applicable labor-hours for all frequencies are to be distributed throughout Levels 2, 3, and 4. A dark gray color represents all frequencies assigned to Level 2.

Level 3, Labor-Hours: Level 3 is considered mission-important. This column includes the total annual PM labor-hour requirements for equipment that falls into this category. As with Level 2 labor-hours, if resources do not allow for the application of total annual labor-hours for Level 3, users may apply the annual and semi-annual frequency labor-hour requirements. This category may also include labor-hours for semi-annual and quarterly, or just quarterly frequencies, that may have annual, or annual and semi-annual, frequency labor-hours in category Level 2. It is important to note that the applicable labor-hours for all frequencies are to be distributed throughout Levels 3 and 4. A light gray color represents all frequencies assigned to Level 3.

Level 4, Labor-Hours: Level 4 equipment maintenance is considered significant but not as crucial as Level 3. This column includes the total annual PM labor-hour requirements for equipment that falls into this category. Level 4 may also include labor-hours for semi-annual, quarterly, and monthly, or just quarterly or monthly frequencies, that may have annual, semi-annual, or quarterly frequency labor-hours in category Level 2 and/or 3. Level 4 is represented in light blue.

10 **Assignment of Labor-Hour Frequencies to Levels** *(Fire Alarm Annunciator System: Level 1 = 11.050, Level 2 = 0, Level 3 = 0, Level 4 = 0)*: The number in each level column across from each equipment type represents the total labor-hours for the frequencies assigned to the equipment in that building model.

11 **Labor-Hours by Shop** *(Fire Protection Shop Labor-Hours: Level 1 = 28.025, Level 2 = 0, Level 3 = 0, Level 4 = 0)*: The number in each level column, across from each shop, represents the total labor-hours for the levels for all the equipment assigned to that shop.

12 **Compiled Labor-Hours** *(Level 1 = 38.248)*: The cumulative total of the total-labor-hours for the levels in that group. The compiled labor-hours for Level 1 are the total labor hours in the Level 1 column. The compiled labor-hours for Level 2 are the sum of the total labor-hours in the Level 1 and Level 2 columns. The compiled labor-hours for Level 3 are the sum of the total labor-hours in the Level 1, 2, and 3 columns. The compiled labor-hours for Level 4 are the sum of the total labor-hours in the Level 1, 2, 3, and 4 columns. These numbers can be used to determine the total amount of PM that can be initiated in a 90,000 square foot classroom building, for example, if resources were available to cover all significant items.

13 **Compiled Labor-Hours per 10,000 SF** *(Level 1 = 4.2)*: The compiled labor-hours per 10,000 square feet of building represent the cumulative total of the total labor-hours for the levels in that group. The compiled labor-hours for Level 1 are the total labor-hours in the Level 1 column divided by 10,000. The compiled labor-hours for Level 2 are the sum of the total labor-hours in the Level 1 and Level 2 columns divided by 10,000. The compiled labor-hours for Level 3 are the sum of the total labor-hours in the Level 1, 2, and 3 columns, divided by 10,000. The compiled labor-hours for Level 4 are the sum of the total labor-hours in the Level 1, 2, 3, and 4 columns, divided by 10,000. These numbers can be used to determine the amount of PM that can be initiated per 10,000 square foot of classroom for a given set of resources, for example.

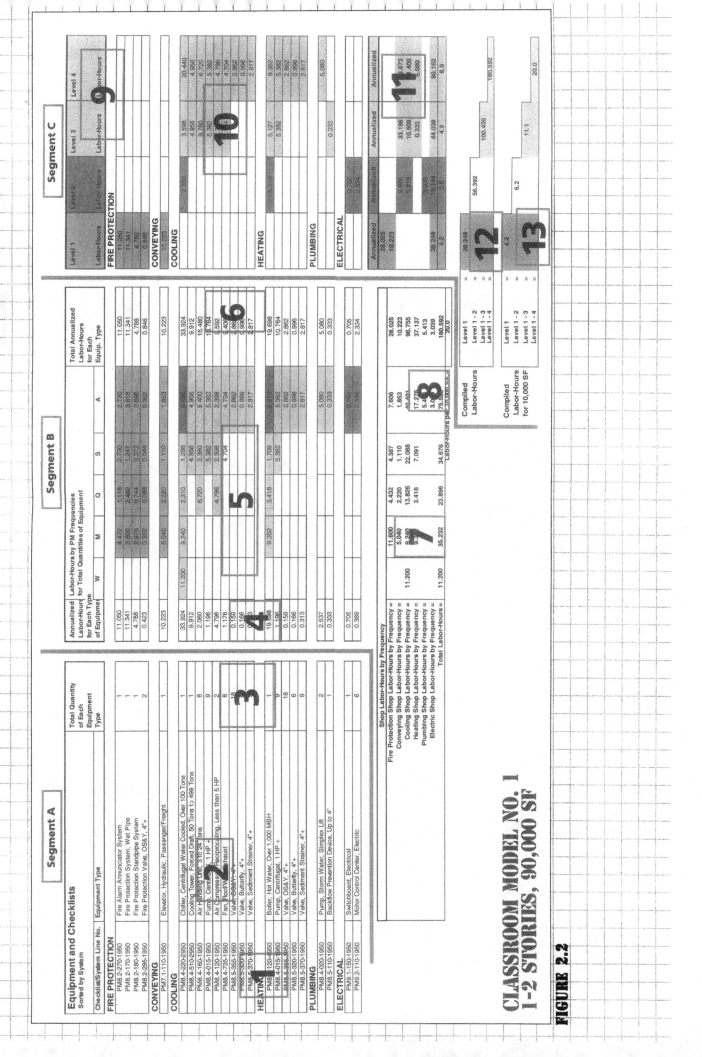

CLASSROOM MODEL NO. 1
1-2 STORIES, 90,000 SF

FIGURE 2.2

21

Application Techniques

This book can serve as a guide to developing a realistic cost of a PM program for a typical campus. The following steps demonstrate the process to determine the labor-hour requirements for a successful program for a single building, followed by an entire campus.

Application to a Single Building

Step 1

Select a building on the campus that closely aligns with one of the building models that follow in this section of the publication. (See Figure 2.3 for an example.)

Step 2

Apply the labor-hour requirements per 10,000 SF of the model to the example building. This will result in the labor-hour requirement for that facility. See Figure 2.4.

The labor-hour requirements are calculated as follows:

$$\frac{\text{(Model Labor-Hours Per 10K SF) (Actual Building SF)}}{10,000 \text{ SF}} = \text{Labor-Hour Requirements}$$

Actual Building: $\dfrac{(21.1)(48,750)}{10,000} = 103$ Hours (Rounded)

Model	Size (SF)	Example Building	Size (SF)
Performing Arts Building	50,000	Shakespeare Theater	48,750

FIGURE 2.3 *Selected Building Example*

Model	Size (SF)	Labor-Hours per 10K SF	Actual Building	Size (SF)	Labor-Hour Requirements
Performing Arts Building	50,000	21.1	Shakespeare Theater	48,750	103
				Total Labor-Hours =	103

FIGURE 2.4 *Labor-Hours for Selected Building Example*

The labor-hour requirements can be further refined by separating them into trades, by simply applying the same process to the shop labor-hours. See Figure 2.5.

Step 3

Apply the labor-hour requirements of the model to Levels 1, 2, 3, and 4. This will allow the user with limited resources to apply a phased approach to the PM program. See Figure 2.6.

The labor-hour requirements for each level is calculated as follows:

$$\frac{\text{(Rounded Model Labor-Hour for Level) (Actual Building SF)}}{\text{SF of the Model}} = \text{Level Labor-Hours (Rounded)}$$

$$\text{Actual Building Level 1: } \frac{(42)\,(48,750)}{50,000} = 41 \text{ Hours}$$

Application to an Entire Campus

Step 1

Separate the different buildings on campus into groups that closely align with the building models that follow in this section of the book. Combining similar buildings into groups will result in a more accurate cost estimate. (See Figure 2.7 for an example.)

Application of Facilities by Group and Shops

Model: Performing Arts Building @ 50,000 SF
Example Building: Shakespeare Theater @ 48,750 SF

Craft	Annualized Labor-Hours	Labor-Hours per 10,000 SF	Example Building Annualized Labor-Hours
Fire Protection Shop Labor-Hours by Frequency =	32.229	6.4	31.2
Conveying Shop Labor-Hours by Frequency =	10.223	2.0	9.8
Heating and Cooling Shop Labor-Hours by Frequency =	39.272	7.9	38.5
Plumbing Shop Labor-Hours by Frequency =	0.333	0.1	0.5
Electric Shop Labor-Hours by Frequency =	23.346	4.7	22.9
Total Labor-Hours =	105.403	21.1	103

FIGURE 2.5 *Craft Labor-Hours for Selected Building Example*

Step 2

Apply the labor-hour estimates per 10,000 SF to the different groups. This will result in the labor-hour requirements for all the selected facilities and each group of facilities. (See Figure 2.8 for an example.)

The 5,864 labor-hour requirement represents the total requirements of all combined trades for the actual buildings used in this example.

Step 3

The labor-hour requirements can be further refined by separating them into levels and applying the same three-step process to the buildings in each group. (See Figure 2.9 for an example.)

The concept of using a phased approach is effective when the user has limited resources, as it prioritizes the most critical types of equipment to include in the PM program. Segment C of the PM models allows users to apply a progressive process in selecting the level of PM that is applied to the equipment. The frequency that is assigned to a PM task is directly related to the impact that the failure of a component has to the continued operation of that

Model	Size (SF)	Level 1	Level 2	Level 3	Level 4
Performing Arts Building	50,000				
Level 1	=	42			
Level 1 - 2	=		49		
Level 1 - 3	=			73	
Level 1 - 4	=				105

Actual Building	Size (SF)	Level 1	Level 2	Level 3	Level 4
Shakespeare Theater	48,750				
Level 1	=	41			
Level 1 - 2	=		48		
Level 1 - 3	=			71	
Level 1 - 4	=				103

FIGURE 2.6 *Labor-Hours by Level for Selected Building Example*

Model	Size (SF)	Actual Building	Size (SF)
Classroom Building No. 1	90,000	Dietrick School of Mathematics	64,158
		Whittemore Hall	78,451
		Jenkins Hall	110,000
		Total SF =	**252,609**
Classroom Building No. 2	240,000	Pritchard School of Education	225,423
		Eastman Building	265,500
		Total SF =	**490,923**
Dormitory Building No. 1	50,000	Barringer Dormitory	57,649
		Vawter Dormitory	78,550
		Total SF =	**136,199**
Dormitory Building No. 2	170,000	Washington Hall	119,000
		Johnson Hall	177,523
		Total SF =	**296,523**
Gymnasium Building No. 1	20,000	Williams Hall	15,654
		Total SF =	**15,654**
Gymnasium Building No. 2	120,000	Price Hall	198,700
		Total SF =	**198,700**
Laboratory Building No. 1	45,000	Means Hall	49,525
		Burruss Hall	56,841
		Total SF =	**106,366**
Laboratory Building No. 2	100,000	Lynnhaven Lab	157,413
		Baker Science Bldg	98,457
		Total SF =	**255,870**
Library Building No. 1	60,000	Owens Hall	27,589
		Total SF =	**27,589**
Library Building No. 2	400,000	Newman Law Library	365,000
		Total SF =	**365,000**
Administration Building No. 1	60,000	Clark Building	45,214
		Rice Housing	78,451
		Total SF =	**123,665**
Administration Building No. 2	100,000	Chesapeake Building	78,900
		Jones Administration Bldg	97,532
		Total SF =	**176,432**
Performing Arts Building	50,000	Shakespeare Theater	48,750
		Total SF =	**48,750**
		Total SF for selected Facilities =	**2,494,280**

FIGURE 2.7 *Combining Like Buildings into Groups*

Model	Size (SF)	Labor-Hours per 10K SF	Actual Building	Size (SF)	Labor-Hour Requirements
Classroom Building No. 1	90,000	20	Dietrick School of Mathematics	64,158	128
			Whittemore Hall	78,451	157
			Jenkins Hall	110,000	220
			Total Labor-Hours =		**505**
Classroom Building No. 2	240,000	10.1	Pritchard School of Education	225,423	228
			Eastman Building	265,500	268
			Total Labor-Hours =		**496**
Dormitory Building No. 1	50,000	36.5	Barringer Dormitory	57,649	210
			Vawter Dormitory	78,550	287
			Total Labor-Hours =		**497**
Dormitory Building No. 2	170,000	18.2	Washington Hall	119,000	217
			Johnson Hall	177,523	323
			Total Labor-Hours =		**540**
Gymnasium Building No. 1	20,000	48.9	Williams Hall	15,654	77
			Total Labor-Hours =		**77**
Gymnasium No. 2	120,000	27.2	Price Hall	198,700	540
			Total Labor-Hours =		**540**
Laboratory Building No. 1	45,000	49.8	Means Hall	49,525	247
			Burruss Hall	56,841	283
			Total Labor-Hours =		**530**
Laboratory Building No.2	100,000	53.4	Lynnhaven Lab	157,413	841
			Baker Science Bldg	98,457	526
			Total Labor-Hours =		**1,366**
Library Building No. 1	60,000	34	Owens Hall	27,589	94
			Total Labor-Hours =		**94**
Library Building No.2	400,000	7.8	Newman Law Library	365,000	285
			Total Labor-Hours =		**285**
Administration Building No. 1	60,000	15.9	Clark Building	45,214	72
			Rice Housing	78,451	125
			Total Labor-Hours =		**197**
Administration Building No. 2	100,000	36	Chesapeake Building	78,900	284
			Jones Administration Bldg	97,532	351
			Total Labor-Hours =		**635**
Performing Arts Building	50,000	21	Shakespeare Theater	48,750	102
			Total Labor-Hours =		**102**
			Total Labor-Hours for Selected Facilities =		5,864

FIGURE 2.8 *Applying Labor-Hours to Groups*

Model	Size (SF)	Labor-Hours per 10K SF	Actual Building by Groups	Size (SF)	Labor-Hour Requirements	Labor-Hours by Levels			
						1	2	3	4
Classroom Building No. 1	90,000	20	Dietrick School of Mathematics	64,158	128.3	26.9	12.8	31.4	57.1
			Whittemore Hall	78,451	156.9	32.9	15.7	38.4	69.8
			Jenkins Hall	110,000	220.0	46.2	22.0	53.9	97.9
			Total Labor-Hours =		505.2				
				Level 1 =		106.1			
				Level 2 =			50.5		
				Level 3 =				123.8	
				Level 4 =					224.8
Classroom Building No. 2	240,000	10.1	Pritchard School of Education	225,423	227.7	63.1	18.0	54.1	92.4
			Eastman Building	265,500	268.2	74.3	21.2	63.7	108.9
			Total Labor-Hours =		495.8				
				Level 1 =		137.5			
				Level 2 =			39.3		
				Level 3 =				117.8	
				Level 4 =					201.3
Dormitory Building No. 1	50,000	36.5	Barringer Dormitory	57,649	210.4	44.4	30.0	43.2	92.8
			Vawter Dormitory	78,550	286.7	60.5	40.8	58.9	126.5
			Total Labor-Hours =		497.1				
				Level 1 =		104.9			
				Level 2 =			70.8		
				Level 3 =				102.1	
				Level 4 =					219.3
Dormitory Building No. 2	170,000	18.2	Washington Hall	119,000	216.6	98.8	20.2	39.3	58.3
			Johnson Hall	177,523	323.1	147.3	30.2	58.6	87.0
			Total Labor-Hours =		539.7				
				Level 1 =		246.1			
				Level 2 =			50.4		
				Level 3 =				97.9	
				Level 4 =					145.3
Gymnasium Building No. 1	20,000	48.9	Williams Hall	15,654	76.5	29.4	3.3	18.5	25.4
			Total Labor-Hours =		76.5				
				Level 1 =		29.4			
				Level 2 =			3.3		
				Level 3 =				18.5	
				Level 4 =					25.4
Gymnasium Building No. 2	120,000	27.2	Price Hall	198,700	540.5	111.3	65.6	125.2	238.4
			Total Labor-Hours =		540.5				
				Level 1 =		111.3			
				Level 2 =			65.6		
				Level 3 =				125.2	
				Level 4 =					238.4
Laboratory Building No. 1	45,000	49.8	Means Hall	49,525	246.6	36.6	13.9	67.8	128.3
			Burruss Hall	56,841	283.1	42.1	15.9	77.9	147.2
			Total Labor-Hours =		529.7				

FIGURE 2.9 *Labor-Hours by Levels for Building Groups Example*

equipment and the mission of the facility. The greater the impact, the more frequent that inspection is required of the components. The equipment frequencies have been evaluated and assigned to different classification levels based on the importance of the equipment to the mission of the facility.

To apply these concepts, users have several options. For example, they could include the labor-hours of the different equipment frequencies starting at Level 1 and continuing through Level 4 until the resource limit has been reached. Another user may decide to fully implement the PM program for a single building, and add other buildings as resources permit. But, the primary purpose of the calculations up to this point is the determination of FTEs.

Converting the PM requirements for the facility and equipment inventory into Full-Time Equivalents (FTEs) personnel is a critical part of selling the need for a PM program. Assume the university has set the definition for an FTE at 1,800 hours. (Note: FTE hours are generally set by college/university administration policy. A full work year of 2,080 hours is reduced for overhead requirements such as vacation, sick time, holidays, training, and so forth.). Referring to Figure 2.8, which shows the number of buildings aligned with the models for the entire campus and the labor-hours associated with the different levels, the 5,864 hours represent approximately 3.25 FTEs (5,864/1,800 hours). How these hours, or FTEs, are distributed, by building, system, equipment, or level, will be determined by the facility manager during actual implementation.

Customizing the Models

The model adjustment approach is a more comprehensive method for determining the user's PM program labor-hour requirements, but can be time-consuming. Individual models are adjusted to more closely reflect the facilities on the user's campus. This degree of customization may or may not be required to successfully sell the PM program to administrators and governing boards.

Select a closely aligned model for each building and customize it to fit the equipment contained in the particular building. Customizing a model may involve adding or deleting equipment to the given building model, or adjusting the quantity of equipment to match the actual building equipment inventory. The example in Figure 2.10 depicts possible changes to a standard model to bring it more in line with the user's building.

Further refinement can be achieved by modifying the PM Standards/Checklists of various pieces of equipment (see Part Three of this book). Tasks can be added, modified, deleted, or re-assigned to different frequencies. These changes will affect the actual building model labor-hour requirements. Figure 2.11 depicts possible changes to an equipment PM Standard/Checklist to better suit the actual requirements of a specific type of equipment.

All models can be customized in an electronic spreadsheet format, downloadable from the book's Website at the following address:

http://www.rsmeans.com/supplement/pmhighed.html

Users can change the quantities, add or subtract equipment, change checkpoints, and modify frequencies.

The next section presents detailed descriptions of the thirteen building models, including the equipment and systems in each and a sample illustration. This section is organized by building type: administration, classroom, gymnasium, and so forth. Each building type contains two models—a sample small and large facility. *(Note: The Performing Arts Center only has one model.)*

It is also important to note that for each of the thirteen models, the annual start-up and shut-down of the air conditioning chiller, cooling tower, and heating system boiler are not included in this publication. This kind of work is intrusive and generally considered recurring maintenance, not PM.

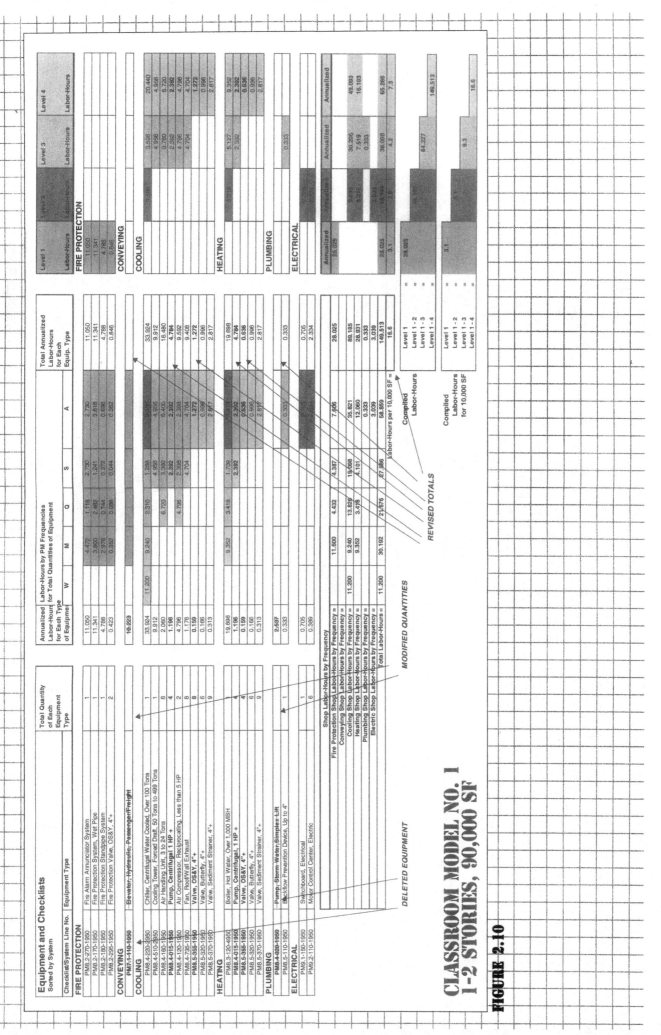

CLASSROOM MODEL NO. 1
1-2 STORIES, 90,000 SF

FIGURE 2.10

31

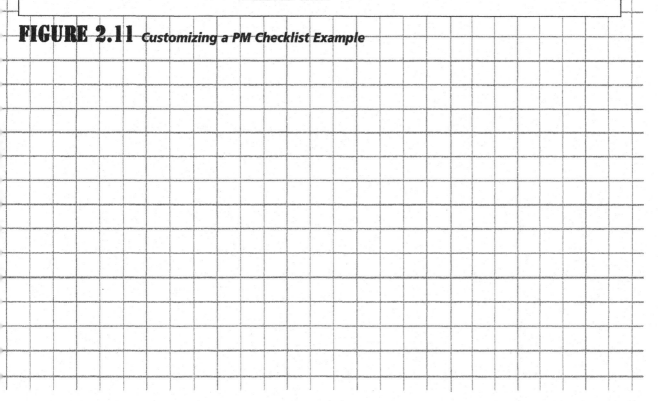

PM8.4-160-1950
AIR HANDLING UNIT, 3 TO 24 TONS

RESULTING CHANGES

	LABOR-HRS	W	M	Q	S	A
				PM FREQUENCY		
Total labor-hours per event		0.000	0.000	0.343	0.343	0.723
Total labor-hours/year by frequency		0.000	0.000	0.686	0.343	0.723
Total labor-hours/year						1.752
1 Check with operating or area personnel for deficiencies.	0.035			X	X	X
2 Check controls and unit for proper operation.	0.033			X	X	X
3 Check for unusual noise or vibration.	0.033			X	X	X
4 Check tension, condition and alignment of belts; adjust as necessary.	0.029			X	X	X
5 Clean coils, evaporator drain pan, blower, motor and drain piping, as required.	0.380					X
6 Lubricate shaft and motor bearings.	0.047			X	X	X
7 Replace air filters.	0.078			X	X	X
8 Inspect exterior piping and valves for leaks; tighten connections as required.	0.077			X	X	X
9 Clean area around equipment.	0.066			X	X	X
10 Fill out maintenance checklist and report deficiencies.	0.022			X	X	X

DELETED TASK

FIGURE 2.11 *Customizing a PM Checklist Example*

ADMINISTRATION BUILDING MODELS

Administration Model #1: 1-2 Stories, 60,000 SF

This model is a two-story, concrete and masonry structure that houses administration and staff offices.

Electrical

The electrical system includes an 800-amp, 277/480-volt, three-phase main switchboard; three motor control centers for equipment; and several 120/208-volt panels and dry-type transformers for general lighting and power. Lighting is supplied by a combination of incandescent, fluorescent, HID, and exit fixtures.

The facility has a fire alarm annunciator system with smoke detectors and pull stations. A 60 kVA generator with an automatic transfer switch supplies power to emergency systems throughout the building. Other electrical systems include the intercom, data, cable television, and telephone systems.

Mechanical

The mechanical systems include heating, air conditioning, ventilation, sanitary, domestic water, fire protection, and one elevator. Cooling and heating are supplied by six 25-ton rooftop package units with gas heaters. Air distribution and ventilation are provided via metal-insulated ducts connected to the rooftop package units and fans. An air compressor supplies control air for the pneumatic environmental control system. Localized gas hot water heaters supply domestic hot water to the restrooms. A wet pipe sprinkler system meets the building's fire protection requirements. A hydraulic elevator provides service between the first and second floors.

*Administration
Model #2:
3-6 Stories,
100,000 SF*

This building model is a six-story, concrete and masonry structure used as an office for several departments and student activity centers.

Electrical

This building's system includes a 2,500-amp, 277/480-volt, three-phase main switchboard; four motor control centers for controlling equipment; and several 277/480-volt and 120/208-volt panels for lighting and power. Lighting is supplied by a combination of incandescent, fluorescent, HID, and exit fixtures. The facility has a fire alarm annunciator system with smoke detectors and pull stations. A 150 kVA generator with an automatic transfer switch supplies power to the building's emergency systems. The facility also contains intercom, data, cable television, and telephone systems.

Mechanical

The mechanical systems for this larger administration building include heating, air conditioning, ventilation, sanitary, domestic water, fire protection, and elevators. Cooling is supplied by a 400-ton centrifugal chiller, a 400-ton cooling tower, a chilled water distribution system, and two 25-ton package computer room units. A 1,200 MBH natural gas-fired hot water boiler and heating hot water distribution system meet the building's heating requirements. Air distribution and ventilation are provided via metal-insulated ducts connected to air handling units and fans, and an air compressor supplies control air for the pneumatic environmental control system. Localized electric hot water heaters supply domestic hot water to the restrooms and teachers' lounges. The fire protection system consists of a standpipe and wet pipe sprinkler system. The facility also has two duplex lift stations for removal of ground and storm water. Two electric traction elevators provide service between the first and sixth floors.

Equipment and Checklists Sorted by System

Checklist/System Line No.	Equipment Type	Total Quantity of Each Equipment Type	Annualized Labor-Hours for Each Type of Equipment	W	M	Q	S	A	Total Annualized Labor-Hours for Each Equipment Type
FIRE PROTECTION									
PM8.2-270-1950	Fire Alarm Annunciator System	1	11.050		4.472	1.118	2.730	2.730	11.050
PM8.2-170-1950	Fire Protection System, Wet Pipe	1	11.341		3.800	2.482	1.241	3.818	11.341
PM8.2-295-1950	Fire Protection Valve, OS&Y, 4"+	2	0.423		0.352	0.088	0.044	0.362	0.846
CONVEYING									
PM7.1-110-1950	Elevator, Hydraulic, Passenger/Freight	1	10.223		5.040	2.220	1.110	1.853	10.223
COOLING AND HEATING									
PM8.4-850-1950	Package/Rooftop Unit, with Duct Gas Heater	6	4.962			9.468	4.734	15.570	29.772
PM8.4-120-1950	Air Compressor, Reciprocating, Less than 5 HP	1	4.796			2.398	1.199	1.199	4.796
PM8.4-736-1950	Fan, Roof/Wall Exhaust	3	1.176				1.764	1.764	3.528
PLUMBING									
PM8.5-110-1950	Backflow Prevention Device, Up To 4"	1	0.333					0.333	0.333
ELECTRICAL									
PM9.1-150-1950	Switchboard, Electrical	1	0.705					0.705	0.705
PM9.2-110-1950	Motor Control Center, Electric	3	0.389				1.167		1.167
PM9.3-105-2950	Generator, Emergency Diesel, Over 15 kVA	1	16.158		10.216	2.554		3.388	16.158
PM9.1-210-1950	Automatic Transfer Switch	1	5.316		3.544	0.886		0.886	5.316

Shop Labor-Hours by Frequency

	M	Q	S	A	Annualized
Fire Protection Shop Labor-Hours by Frequency =	8.624	3.688	4.015	6.910	23.237
Conveying Shop Labor-Hours by Frequency =	5.040	2.220	1.110	1.853	10.223
Heating and Cooling Shop Labor-Hours by Frequency =		11.866	7.697	18.533	38.096
Plumbing Shop Labor-Hours by Frequency =				0.333	0.333
Electric Shop Labor-Hours by Frequency =	13.760	3.440	1.720	4.426	23.346
Total Labor-Hours =	27.424	21.214	14.542	32.055	95.235

Labor-Hours per 10,000 SF = 15.9

Compiled Labor-Hours

Level 1	33.460
Level 1 - 2	
Level 1 - 3	63.111
Level 1 - 4	95.235

Compiled Labor-Hours for 10,000 SF

Level 1	5.6
Level 1 - 2	
Level 1 - 3	10.5
Level 1 - 4	15.9

Labor-Hours by Level

	Level 1	Level 2	Level 3	Level 4
FIRE PROTECTION	11.050 / 11.341 / 0.846			
CONVEYING	10.223			
COOLING AND HEATING			15.570 / 2.398 / 1.764	14.202 / 2.398 / 1.764
PLUMBING			0.333	
ELECTRICAL		0.705 / 1.167	2.554 / 0.596	10.216 / 3.544

ADMINISTRATION MODEL NO. 1
1-2 STORIES, 60,000 SF

ADMINISTRATION MODEL, NO. 2
3-6 STORIES, 100,000 SF

Equipment and Checklists — Sorted by System

Checklist/System Line No.	Equipment Type	Total Quantity of Each Equipment Type	Annualized Labor-Hours for Each Type of Equipment	W	M	Q	S	A	Total Annualized Labor-Hours for Each Equipment Type
FIRE PROTECTION									
PM8.2-270-1950	Fire Alarm Annunciator System	1	11.050	4.472	1.118	2.730		2.730	11.050
PM8.2-170-1950	Fire Protection System, Wet Pipe	1	11.341	3.800	2.482	1.241		3.818	11.341
PM8.2-180-1950	Fire Protection Standpipe System	1	4.788	2.976	0.744	0.372		0.698	4.788
PM8.2-295-1950	Fire Protection Valve, OS&Y, 4"+	7	0.423	1.232	0.308	0.154		1.267	2.961
CONVEYING									
PM7.1-210-1950	Elevator, Cable, Electric, Passenger/Freight	2	47.613		48.976	20.076	10.038	16.136	95.226
COOLING									
PM8.4-220-2950	Chiller, Centrifugal Water Cooled, Over 100 Tons	1	33.924	11.200	9.240	2.310	1.288	9.886	33.924
PM8.4-510-2950	Cooling Tower, Forced Draft, 50 to 499 Tons	1	9.912		4.956			4.956	9.912
PM8.4-160-2950	Air Handling Unit 25 to 50 Tons	3	2.138		2.520	1.260		2.634	6.414
PM8.4-160-1950	Air Handling Unit, 3 to 24 Tons	2	2.060		1.680	0.840		1.600	4.120
PM8.4-840-1950	Package Unit, Computer Room	2	4.336		3.036	2.818		2.818	8.672
PM8.4-760-1950	Fluid Cooler, 2 Fans	2	1.123					2.246	2.246
PM8.4-015-1950	Pump, Centrifugal, 1 HP+	5	1.196		2.990			2.990	5.980
PM8.4-120-2950	Air Compressor, Reciprocating, 5 to 40 HP	2	4.856		4.856	2.428		2.428	9.712
PM8.4-735-1950	Fan, Roof/Wall Exhaust	6	1.176			3.528		3.528	7.056
PM8.4-710-3950	Fan, Axial, 36" to 48" Dia (Over 10,000 CFM)	3	1.390			2.085		2.085	4.170
PM8.5-365-1950	Valve, OS&Y, 4"+	10	0.159					1.590	1.590
PM8.5-320-1950	Valve, Butterfly, 4"+	6	0.166					0.996	0.996
PM8.5-370-1950	Valve, Sediment Strainer, 4"+	3	0.313					0.939	0.939
HEATING									
PM8.3-120-4950	Boiler, Hot Water, Over 1,000 MBH	1	19.698		9.352	3.418	1.709	5.219	19.698
PM8.4-015-1950	Pump, Centrifugal, 1 HP+	5	1.196		2.990			2.990	5.980
PM8.5-365-1950	Valve, OS&Y, 4"+	14	0.159					2.226	2.226
PM8.5-370-1950	Valve, Sediment Strainer, 4"+	3	0.313					0.939	0.939
PLUMBING									
PM8.5-110-1950	Backflow Prevention Device, Up to 4"	1	0.333					0.333	0.333
PM8.4-020-2950	Pump, Storm Water, Duplex Lift	2	4.196		4.196			4.196	8.392
PM8.5-365-1950	Valve, OS&Y, 4"+	4	0.159					0.636	0.636
ELECTRICAL									
PM9.1-160-1950	Switchboard, Electrical	1	0.705					0.705	0.705
PM9.2-110-1950	Motor Control Center, Electric	4	0.389					1.556	1.556
PM9.3-170-2950	Uninterruptible Power System, 200 to 800 kVA	1	78.084		40.352	18.866	9.433	9.433	78.084
PM9.3-105-2950	Generator, Emergency Diesel, Over 15 kVA	1	16.158		10.216	2.554	1.277	2.111	16.158
PM9.1-210-1950	Automatic Transfer Switch	1	5.316		3.544	0.886	0.443	0.443	5.316

Shop Labor-Hours by Frequency

	W	M	Q	S	A	Total Labor-Hours
Fire Protection Shop Labor-Hours by Frequency =	12.480	4.652	4.497		8.511	30.140
Conveying Shop Labor-Hours by Frequency =		48.976	20.076	10.038	16.136	95.226
Cooling Shop Labor-Hours by Frequency =	11.200	9.240	14.402	22.193	38.696	95.731
Heating Shop Labor-Hours by Frequency =		9.352	3.418	4.699	11.374	28.843
Plumbing Shop Labor-Hours by Frequency =		10.216	2.564	1.277	2.111	9.361
Electric Shop Labor-Hours by Frequency =	3.544	54.112	22.306	11.153	14.248	101.819
Total Shop Labor-Hours by Frequency =	11.200	54.112	134.160	64.854	98.326	361.120
Total Labor-Hours by Frequency =						
Labor-Hours per 10,000 SF =					52.580	36.0

Total Annualized Labor-Hours for Each Equipment Type (by Level)

System	Labor-Hours	Level 1	Level 2	Level 3	Level 4
FIRE PROTECTION					
	11.050	11.050			
	11.341	11.341			
	4.788	4.788			
	2.961	2.961			
CONVEYING	95.226	95.226			
COOLING		9.886		2.818	
	33.924				
HEATING		5.127	5.219		
PLUMBING		0.333			0.333
ELECTRICAL		1.556			

System Annualized Summary

System	Annualized
FIRE PROTECTION	30.140
CONVEYING	95.226
COOLING	95.731
HEATING	28.843
PLUMBING	9.361
ELECTRICAL	101.819

Compiled Labor-Hours

	Compiled Labor-Hours	Compiled Labor-Hours for 10,000 SF
Level 1	125.4	12.5
Level 1 - 2	188.7	15.8
Level 1 - 3	232.9	23.2
Level 1 - 4	361.1	36.0

CLASSROOM BUILDING MODELS

Classroom Model #1: 1-2 Stories, 90,000 SF

The first facility is a two-story, concrete and masonry structure used as a classroom building.

Electrical

The electrical systems include a 1,200-amp, 277/480-volt, three-phase main switchboard; six motor control centers for controlling equipment; and several 277/480-volt and 120/208-volt panels for lighting and power. Lighting is supplied by a combination of incandescent, fluorescent, HID, and exit fixtures. The facility has a fire alarm annunciator system with smoke detectors and pull stations. Other electrical systems include intercom, data, cable television, and telephone systems.

Mechanical

The facility's mechanical systems include heating, air conditioning, ventilation, sanitary, domestic water, fire protection, and one elevator. Cooling is supplied by a 200-ton centrifugal chiller, a 200-ton cooling tower, and a chilled water distribution system. Heating

is provided by a 1,200 MBH natural gas-fired hot water boiler and a heating hot water distribution system. Air distribution and ventilation are supplied via metal-insulated ducts connected to air handling units and fans. An air compressor provides control air for the pneumatic environmental control system. Localized electric hot water heaters supply domestic hot water to the restrooms and teachers' lounges. A standpipe and wet pipe sprinkler system meet the building's fire protection requirements. The facility also has a simplex lift station for removal of ground and storm water. A hydraulic elevator provides service between the first and second floors.

Classroom Model #2: 2-4 Stories, 240,000 SF

This larger classroom model is a four-story, concrete and masonry structure.

Electrical

The building's electrical systems include a 3,000-amp, 277/480-volt, three-phase main switchboard; four motor control centers for equipment; and several 277/480-volt and 120/208-volt panels for lighting and power. Lighting is supplied by a combination of incandescent, fluorescent, HID, and exit fixtures. The facility has a fire alarm annunciator system with smoke detectors and pull stations. Other electrical systems include intercom, data, cable television, and telephone.

Mechanical

This classroom building's mechanical systems include heating, air conditioning, ventilation, sanitary, domestic water, fire protection, and elevators. Cooling is supplied by a 400-ton centrifugal chiller, a 400-ton cooling tower, and a chilled water distribution system. The heating system consists of an 1,800 MBH natural gas-fired steam boiler, heat exchangers, and a heating hot water distribution system. Air distribution and ventilation are provided via metal-insulated ducts connected to air handling units and fans. An air compressor supplies control air for the pneumatic environmental control system. Localized electric hot water heaters provide domestic hot water to the restrooms and lounges. A standpipe system and wet pipe sprinkler system serve as the building's fire protection system. The facility also has a duplex lift station for removal of ground and storm water. Two hydraulic elevators provide service between the first and fourth floors.

Equipment and Checklists
Sorted by System

Checklist/System Line No.	Equipment Type	Total Quantity of Each Equipment Type	Annualized Labor-Hours for Each Type of Equipment	W	M	Q	S	A	Total Annualized Labor-Hours for Each Equip. Type	Level 1 Labor-Hours	Level 2 Labor-Hours	Level 3 Labor-Hours	Level 4 Labor-Hours
FIRE PROTECTION													
PM8.2-270-1950	Fire Alarm Annunciator System	1	11.050		4.472	1.118	2.730	2.730	11.050	11.050			
PM8.2-170-1950	Fire Protection System, Wet Pipe	1	11.341		3.800	2.482	1.241	3.818	11.341	11.341			
PM8.2-180-1950	Fire Protection Standpipe System	1	4.788		2.976	0.744	0.372	0.696	4.788	4.788			
PM8.2-295-1950	Fire Protection Valve, OS&Y, 4"+	2	0.423		0.352	0.088	0.044	0.362	0.846	0.846			
CONVEYING													
PM7.1-110-1950	Elevator, Hydraulic, Passenger/Freight	1	10.223		5.040	2.220	1.110	1.853	10.223	10.223			
COOLING													
PM8.4-220-2950	Chiller, Centrifugal Water Cooled, Over 100 Tons	1	33.924	11.200	9.240	2.310	1.268	9.886	33.924		9.886	3.598	20.440
PM8.4-510-2950	Cooling Tower, Forced Draft, 50 Tons to 499 Tons	1	9.912				4.956	4.956	9.912			4.956	4.956
PM8.4-160-1950	Air Handling Unit, 3 to 24 Tons	8	2.060			6.720	3.360	6.400	16.480			9.760	6.720
PM8.4-015-1950	Pump, Centrifugal, 1 HP+	9	1.196				5.382	5.382	10.764			5.382	5.382
PM8.4-120-1950	Air Compressor, Reciprocating, Less than 5 HP	2	4.796			4.796	2.398	2.398	9.592			4.796	4.796
PM8.4-735-1950	Fan, Roof/Wall Exhaust	8	1.176				4.704	4.704	9.408			4.704	4.704
PM8.5-355-1950	Valve, OS&Y, 4"+	18	0.159					2.862	2.862				2.862
PM8.5-320-1950	Valve, Butterfly, 4"+	6	0.166					0.996	0.996				0.996
PM8.5-370-1950	Valve, Sediment Strainer, 4"+	9	0.313					2.817	2.817				2.817
HEATING													
PM8.3-120-4950	Boiler, Hot Water, Over 1,000 MBH	1	19.698		9.352	3.418	1.709	5.219	19.698		5.219	5.127	9.352
PM8.4-015-1950	Pump, Centrifugal, 1 HP+	9	1.196				5.382	5.382	10.764			5.382	5.382
PM8.5-355-1950	Valve, OS&Y, 4"+	18	0.159					2.862	2.862				2.862
PM8.5-320-1950	Valve, Butterfly, 4"+	6	0.166					0.996	0.996				0.996
PM8.5-370-1950	Valve, Sediment Strainer, 4"+	9	0.313					2.817	2.817				2.817
PLUMBING													
PM8.4-020-1950	Pump, Storm Water, Simplex Lift	2	2.537					5.080	5.080				5.080
PM8.5-110-1950	Backflow Prevention Device, Up to 4"	1	0.333					0.333	0.333			0.333	
ELECTRICAL													
PM9.1-150-1950	Switchboard, Electrical	1	0.705					0.705	0.705		0.705		
PM9.2-110-1950	Motor Control Center, Electric	6	0.389					2.334	2.334		2.334		

Shop Labor-Hours by Frequency

	W	M	Q	S	A	Annualized
Fire Protection Shop Labor-Hours by Frequency =		11.600	4.432	4.387	7.606	28.025
Conveying Shop Labor-Hours by Frequency =		5.040	2.220	1.110	1.853	10.223
Cooling Shop Labor-Hours by Frequency =	11.200	9.240	13.826	22.088	40.401	96.755
Heating Shop Labor-Hours by Frequency =		9.352	3.418	7.091	17.276	37.137
Plumbing Shop Labor-Hours by Frequency =					5.413	5.413
Electric Shop Labor-Hours by Frequency =					3.039	3.039
Total Labor-Hours =	11.200	35.232	23.896	34.676	75.588	180.592

Annualized by Level

	Level 1 Annualized	Level 2 Annualized	Level 3 Annualized	Level 4 Annualized
Fire Protection	28.025			
Conveying	10.223			
Cooling		9.886	33.196	53.673
Heating		5.219	10.509	21.409
Plumbing			0.333	5.080
Electrical		3.039		
Total	38.248	18.144	44.038	80.162
Labor-Hours per 10,000 SF	4.2	2.0	4.9	8.9

Compiled Labor-Hours

	Compiled Labor-Hours	Compiled Labor-Hours for 10,000 SF
Level 1	38.248	4.2
Level 1 - 2	56.392	6.2
Level 1 - 3	100.430	11.1
Level 1 - 4	180.592	20.0

CLASSROOM MODEL NO. 1
1-2 STORIES, 90,000 SF

CLASSROOM MODEL, NO. 2 — 2-4 STORIES, 240,000 SF

Equipment and Checklists
Sorted by System

Checklist/System Line No.	Equipment Type	Total Quantity of Each Equipment Type	Annualized Labor-Hours for Each Equipment	W	M	Q	S	A	Total Annualized Labor-Hours for Each Equipment Type
FIRE PROTECTION									
PM8.2-270-1950	Fire Alarm Annunciator System	1	11.050		4.472	1.118	2.730	2.730	11.050
PM8.2-170-1950	Fire Protection System, Wet Pipe	1	11.341		3.800	2.482	1.241	3.818	11.341
PM8.2-180-1950	Fire Protection Standpipe System	1	4.788		2.976	0.744	0.372	0.696	4.788
PM8.2-250-1950	Fire Pump, Electric	1	16.944		11.296	2.824	1.412	1.412	16.944
PM8.2-295-1950	Fire Protection Valve, OS&Y, 4"+	8	0.423		1.408	0.352	0.176	1.448	3.384
CONVEYING									
PM7.1-110-1950	Elevator, Hydraulic, Passenger/Freight	2	10.223		10.080	4.440	2.220	3.706	20.446
COOLING									
PM8.4-220-2950	Chiller, Centrifugal Water Cooled, Over 100 Tons	1	33.924	11.200				9.886	33.924
PM8.4-510-2960	Cooling Tower, Forced Draft, 50 to 499 Tons	1	9.912						9.912
PM8.4-160-2960	Air Handling Unit, 25 to 50 Tons	6	2.138						12.828
PM8.4-160-1950	Air Handling Unit, 3 to 24 Tons	4	2.060						8.240
PM8.4-015-1950	Pump, Centrifugal, 1 HP +	8	1.196						9.568
PM8.4-120-2950	Air Compressor, Reciprocating, 5 to 40 HP	2	4.856						9.712
PM8.4-735-1950	Fan, Roof/Wall Exhaust	12	1.176				7.056	7.056	14.112
PM8.4-710-3950	Fan, Axial, 36" to 48" Dia (Over 10,000 CFM)	6	1.390				4.170	4.170	8.340
PM8.5-355-1950	Valve, OS&Y, 4"+	16	0.159						2.544
PM8.5-320-1950	Valve, Butterfly, 4"+	8	0.166						1.328
PM8.5-340-1950	Valve, Gate, 4"+	8	0.159						1.272
PM8.5-350-1950	Valve, Motor Operated, 4"+	4	1.002				2.004	2.004	4.008
PM8.5-370-1950	Valve, Sediment Strainer, 4"+	8	0.313					2.504	2.504
HEATING									
PM8.3-160-4950	Boiler, Steam, Over 1000 MBH	1	22.450		8.304	5.290	2.645	6.211	22.450
PM8.4-015-1950	Pump, Centrifugal, 1 HP +	8	1.196				4.784	4.784	9.568
PM8.3-710-3950	Pump, Steam Condensate Return, Duplex	2	1.142				1.142	1.142	2.284
PM8.5-365-1950	Valve, OS&Y, 4"+	16	0.159					2.544	2.544
PM8.5-320-1950	Valve, Butterfly, 4"+	8	0.166					1.328	1.328
PM8.5-340-1950	Valve, Gate, 4"+	8	0.159					1.272	1.272
PM8.5-380-1950	Valve, Motor Operated, 4"+	4	1.002				2.004	2.004	4.008
PM8.5-370-1950	Valve, Sediment Strainer, 4"+	8	0.313					2.504	2.504
PLUMBING									
PM8.5-110-1950	Backflow Prevention Device, Up to 4"	1	0.333					0.333	0.333
PM8.4-020-2950	Pump, Storm Water, Duplex Lift	2	4.196					8.392	8.392
PM8.5-335-1950	Valve, OS&Y, 4"+	4	0.159					0.636	0.636
PM8.5-340-1950	Valve, Gate, 4"+	4	0.159					0.636	0.636
ELECTRICAL									
PM9.1-150-1950	Switchboard, Electrical	1	0.705					0.705	0.705
PM9.2-110-1950	Motor Control Center, Electric	4	0.389					1.556	1.556

Shop Labor-Hours by Frequency

	W	M	Q	S	A	Compiled Labor-Hours
Fire Protection Shop Labor-Hours by Frequency =		23.952	7.520	5.931	10.104	47.507
Conveying Shop Labor-Hours by Frequency =	11.200	10.080	4.440	2.220	3.706	20.446
Cooling Shop Labor-Hours by Frequency =		9.240	15.566	30.886	50.764	117.656
Heating Shop Labor-Hours by Frequency =		8.304	5.290	10.575	21.153	45.322
Plumbing Shop Labor-Hours by Frequency =					9.997	9.997
Electric Shop Labor-Hours by Frequency =					2.261	2.261
Total Labor-Hours =	11.200	51.576	32.816	49.612	97.985	243.189
Labor-Hours per 10,000 SF =						10.1

Total Annualized Labor-Hours for Each Equipment Type — by Level

System	Level 1 Labor-Hours	Level 2 Labor-Hours	Level 3 Labor-Hours	Level 4 Labor-Hours
FIRE PROTECTION	11.050 / 11.341 / 4.788 / 16.944 / 3.384			
CONVEYING	20.446			
COOLING	20.440	9.886	3.598	
HEATING			6.211	
PLUMBING	0.333			
ELECTRICAL	0.705	1.556		

Annualized (cumulative by level)

	Level 1	Level 1-2	Level 1-3	Level 1-4
FIRE PROTECTION	47.507	20.446		
COOLING		9.886	42.088 / 15.003 / 0.333	65.682 / 24.108 / 9.664
HEATING	6.211	6.211	18.358	57.424
PLUMBING	0.333	8.392		
ELECTRICAL	0.705	1.556		
	67.953		99.454	

Compiled Labor-Hours

	Compiled Labor-Hours	for 10,000 SF
Level 1	47.507	
Level 1-2	68.0	2.8
Level 1-3	143.7	6.0
Level 1-4	243.189	10.1

Level 1	2.8
Level 1-2	86.3 / 3.6
Level 1-3	143.7 / 6.0
Level 1-4	243.2 / 10.1

DORMITORY BUILDING MODELS

Dormitory Model #1: 1-3 Stories, 50,000 SF

This building is a three-story, concrete and masonry structure used for student housing. It does not include dining or snack facilities.

Electrical

The building's electrical systems include a 1,200 amp, 120/208-volt, three-phase main switchboard; three motor control centers for equipment; and several panels for lighting and power. Lighting is supplied by a combination of incandescent, fluorescent, HID, and exit fixtures. The facility has a fire alarm annunciator system with smoke detectors and pull stations. A 60 kVA generator with an automatic transfer switch supplies power to the dormitory's emergency systems. The facility also contains data, cable television, and telephone systems.

Mechanical

The dormitory's mechanical systems include heating, air conditioning, ventilation, sanitary, domestic water, fire protection, and an elevator. Cooling is supplied by a 100-ton centrifugal chiller,

a 100-ton cooling tower, and a chilled water distribution system. Heating is provided by a 1,000 MBH natural gas-fired hot water boiler and a heating hot water distribution system. Metal-insulated ducts connected to air handling units and fans are used for air distribution and ventilation, and an air compressor supplies control air for the pneumatic environmental control system. A 750 MBH natural gas-fired hot water boiler supplies domestic hot water to the restrooms and shower areas. Fire protection is provided by a standpipe and wet pipe sprinkler system. A hydraulic elevator provides service between the first and third floors.

Dormitory Model #2: 4-8 Stories, 170,000 SF

The second model is an eight-story, concrete and masonry structure also used for student housing. Dining or snack facilities are not included as part of this model.

Electrical

The electrical systems include a 3,000-amp, 277/480-volt, three-phase main switchboard; six motor control centers for controlling equipment; and several 277/480-volt and 120/208-volt panels for lighting and power. Lighting is supplied by a combination of incandescent, fluorescent, HID, and exit fixtures. The facility also has a fire alarm annunciator system with smoke detectors and pull stations. A 100 kVA generator with an automatic transfer switch supplies power to the building's emergency systems. The facility also contains data, cable television, and telephone systems.

Mechanical

This model's mechanical systems include heating, air conditioning, ventilation, sanitary, domestic water, fire protection, and elevators. Cooling is supplied by a 200-ton centrifugal chiller, a 200-ton cooling tower, and a chilled water distribution system. Heating is provided by an 1,800 MBH natural gas-fired steam boiler, heat exchangers, and a heating hot water distribution system. Metal-insulated ducts connected to air handling units and fans are used for air distribution and ventilation, and an air compressor supplies control air for the pneumatic environmental control system. A 750 MBH natural gas-fired hot water boiler supplies domestic hot water to the restrooms and shower areas.

The facility has a sanitary and domestic water system. Standpipe and wet pipe sprinkler systems serve as the building's fire protection system. The facility has a duplex lift station for removal of ground and storm water. Two electric traction elevators provide service between the first and eighth floors.

DORMITORY MODEL NO. 1
1-3 STORIES, 50,000 SF

Equipment and Checklists — Sorted by System

Checklist/System Line No.	Equipment Type	Total Quantity of Each Equipment Type	Annualized Labor-Hours for Each Type of Equipment	W	M	Q	S	A	Total Annualized Labor-Hours for Each Equipment Type	Level 1 Labor-Hours	Level 2 Labor-Hours	Level 3 Labor-Hours	Level 4 Labor-Hours
FIRE PROTECTION													
PM8.2-270-1950	Fire Alarm Annunciator System	1	11.050		4.472	1.118	2.730	2.730	11.050	11.050			
PM8.2-170-1950	Fire Protection System, Wet Pipe	1	11.341		3.800	2.482	1.241	3.818	11.341	11.341			
PM8.2-180-1950	Fire Protection Standpipe System	1	4.788		2.976	0.744	0.372	0.696	4.788	4.788			
PM8.2-295-1950	Fire Protection Valve, OS&Y, 4"+	3	0.423		0.528	0.132	0.066	0.543	1.269	1.269			
CONVEYING													
PM7.1-110-1950	Elevator, Hydraulic, Passenger/Freight	1	10.223		5.040	2.220	1.110	1.853	10.223	10.223			
COOLING													
PM8.4-220-2950	Chiller, Centrifugal Water Cooled, Over 100 Tons	1	33.924	11.200	9.240	2.310	1.288	9.886	33.924		9.886	3.598	20.440
PM8.4-510-2950	Cooling Tower, Forced Draft, 50 to 499 Tons	1	9.912				4.956	4.956	9.912			4.956	4.956
PM8.4-160-1950	Air Handling Unit, 3 to 24 Tons	5	2.060			4.200	2.100	4.000	10.300			6.100	4.200
PM8.4-015-1950	Pump, Centrifugal, 1 HP +	2	1.196				1.196	1.196	2.392			1.196	1.196
PM8.4-120-1950	Air Compressor, Reciprocating, Less than 5 HP	1	4.796			2.398	1.199	1.199	4.796			2.398	2.398
PM8.4-735-1950	Fan, Roof/Wall Exhaust	6	1.176				3.528	3.528	7.056			3.528	3.528
PM8.5-365-1950	Valve, OS&Y, 4"+	5	0.159					0.795	0.795				0.795
PM8.5-320-1950	Valve, Butterfly, 4"+	3	0.166					0.498	0.498				0.498
PM8.5-350-1950	Valve, Motor Operated, 4"+	3	1.002				1.503	1.503	3.006				3.006
PM8.5-370-1950	Valve, Sediment Strainer, 4"+	2	0.313					0.626	0.626				0.626
HEATING													
PM8.3-120-4950	Boiler, Hot Water, Over 1,000 MBH	1	19.698		9.352	3.418	1.709	5.219	19.698		5.219	5.127	9.352
PM8.4-015-1950	Pump, Centrifugal, 1 HP +	2	1.196				1.196	1.196	2.392			1.196	1.196
PM8.5-355-1950	Valve, OS&Y, 4"+	5	0.159					0.795	0.795				0.795
PM8.5-320-1950	Valve, Butterfly, 4"+	3	0.166					0.498	0.498				0.498
PM8.5-350-1950	Valve, Motor Operated, 4"+	3	1.002				1.503	1.503	3.006				3.006
PM8.5-370-1950	Valve, Sediment Strainer, 4"+	2	0.313					0.626	0.626				0.626
PLUMBING													
PM8.5-110-1950	Backflow Prevention Device, Up to 4"	1	0.333					0.333	0.333			0.333	
PM8.3-120-3950	Boiler, Hot Water, 500 to 1,000 MBH	1	17.378		7.968	2.984	1.492	4.934	17.378		4.934	4.476	7.968
PM8.4-015-1950	Pump, Centrifugal, 1 HP +	2	1.196				1.196	1.196	2.392			1.196	1.196
PM8.5-355-1950	Valve, OS&Y, 4"+	2	0.159					0.318	0.318				0.318
ELECTRICAL													
PM9.1-150-1950	Electrical Switchboard	1	0.705					0.705	0.705		0.705		
PM9.2-110-1950	Electrical Motor Control Center	3	0.389					1.167	1.167		1.167		
PM9.3-105-2950	Generator, Emergency Diesel, Over 15 kVA	1	16.158		10.216	2.554	1.277	2.111	16.158		3.388	2.554	10.216
PM9.1-210-1950	Automatic Transfer Switch	1	5.316		3.544	0.886	0.443	0.443	5.316		0.886	0.886	3.544

Shop Labor-Hours by Frequency

	W	M	Q	S	A	Annualized
Fire Protection Shop Labor-Hours by Frequency =		11.776	4.476	4.409	7.787	28.448
Conveying Shop Labor-Hours by Frequency =		5.040	2.220	1.110	1.853	10.223
Cooling Shop Labor-Hours by Frequency =	11.200	9.240	8.908	15.770	28.187	73.305
Heating Shop Labor-Hours by Frequency =		9.352	3.418	4.408	9.837	27.015
Plumbing Shop Labor-Hours by Frequency =		7.968	2.984	2.688	6.781	20.421
Electric Shop Labor-Hours by Frequency =		13.760	3.440	1.720	4.426	23.346
Total Labor-Hours =	11.200	57.136	25.446	30.105	58.871	182.758

Labor-Hours per 10,000 SF = 36.5

Compiled Labor-Hours

Level 1	=	38.7
Level 1 - 2	=	64.9
Level 1 - 3	=	102.4
Level 1 - 4	=	182.8

Compiled Labor-Hours for 10,000 SF

Level 1	=	7.7
Level 1 - 2	=	12.9
Level 1 - 3	=	20.4
Level 1 - 4	=	36.5

Annualized Labor-Hours by Level

Level	Annualized	per 10,000 SF
Level 1	38.671	7.7
Level 2	26.186	5.2
Level 3	37.544	7.5
Level 4	80.356	16.1

DORMITORY MODEL NO. 2 — 4-8 STORIES, 170,000 SF

Equipment and Checklists (Sorted by System)

Checklist/System Line No.	Equipment Type	Total Quantity of Each Equipment Type	Annualized Labor-Hours for Each Type of Equipment	W	M	Q	S	A	Total Annualized Labor-Hours for Each Equipment Type
FIRE PROTECTION									
PM8.2-270-1950	Fire Alarm Annunciator System	1	11.050		4.472	1.118	2.730	2.730	11.050
PM8.2-170-1950	Fire Protection System, Wet Pipe	1	11.341		3.800	2.482	1.241	3.818	11.341
PM8.2-180-1950	Fire Protection Standpipe System	1	4.788		2.976	0.744	0.372	0.696	4.788
PM8.2-250-1950	Fire Pump, Electric	1	16.944		11.296	2.824	1.412	1.412	16.944
PM8.2-295-1950	Fire Protection Valve, OS&Y, 4"+	5	0.423		0.880	0.220	0.110	0.905	2.115
CONVEYING									
PM7.1-210-1950	Elevator, Cable, Electric, Passenger/Freight	2	47.613		48.976	20.076	10.038	16.136	95.226
COOLING									
PM8.4-220-2950	Chiller, Centrifugal Water Cooled, Over 100 Tons	1	33.924	11.200	9.240	2.310	1.288	9.886	33.924
PM8.4-510-2950	Cooling Tower, Forced Draft, 50 to 499 Tons	1	9.912				4.956	4.956	9.912
PM8.4-160-2950	Air Handling Unit, 25 to 50 Tons	1	2.138			0.840	0.420	0.878	2.138
PM8.4-160-1950	Air Handling Unit, 3 to 24 Tons	5	2.060			4.200	2.100	4.000	10.300
PM8.4-015-1950	Pump, Centrifugal, 1 HP +	4	1.196				2.392	2.392	4.784
PM8.4-120-2950	Air Compressor, Reciprocating, 5 to 40 HP	2	4.856			4.856	2.428	2.428	9.712
PM8.4-735-1950	Fan, Roof/Wall Exhaust	6	1.176				3.528	3.528	7.056
PM8.4-710-3950	Fan, Axial, 36" to 48" Dia (Over 10,000 CFM)	1	1.390				0.695	0.695	1.390
PM8.5-355-1950	Valve, OS&Y, 4"+	10	0.159					1.590	1.590
PM8.5-320-1950	Valve, Butterfly, 4"+	6	0.166					0.996	0.996
PM8.5-370-1950	Valve, Sediment Strainer, 4"+	4	0.313					1.252	1.252
HEATING									
PM8.3-160-4950	Boiler, Steam, Over 1000 MBH	1	22.450		8.304	5.290	2.645	6.211	22.450
PM8.4-015-1950	Pump, Centrifugal, 1 HP +	4	1.196				2.392	2.392	4.784
PM8.3-710-3950	Pump, Steam Condensate Return, Duplex	5	1.142				2.745	2.746	5.490
PM8.5-355-1950	Valve, OS&Y, 4"+	4	0.159					0.636	0.636
PM8.5-320-1950	Valve, Butterfly, 4"+	10	0.166					1.660	1.660
PM8.5-370-1950	Valve, Sediment Strainer, 4"+	4	0.313					1.252	1.252
PLUMBING									
PM8.3-120-3950	Boiler, Hot Water, 500 to 1,000 MBH	1	17378.000		7.968	2.984	1.492	4.934	17.378
PM8.4-015-1950	Pump, Centrifugal, 1 HP +	2	1.196				1.196	1.196	2.392
PM8.4-020-2950	Pump, Storm Water, Duplex Lift	1	4.196					4.196	4.196
PM8.5-110-1950	Backflow Prevention Device, Up to 4"	1	0.333					0.333	0.333
PM8.5-355-1950	Valve, OS&Y, 4"+	4	0.159					0.636	0.636
ELECTRICAL									
PM9.1-150-1950	Electrical Switchboard	1	0.705					0.705	0.705
PM9.2-110-1950	Electrical Motor Control Center	6	0.389					2.334	2.334
PM9.3-105-2950	Generator, Emergency Diesel, Over 15 kVA	1	16.158		10.216	2.554	1.277	2.111	16.158
PM9.1-210-1950	Automatic Transfer Switch	1	5.316		3.544	0.886	0.443	0.443	5.316

Annualized Labor-Hours by Level

Equipment Type	Level 1	Level 2	Level 3	Level 4
FIRE PROTECTION				
Fire Alarm Annunciator System	11.050			
Fire Protection System, Wet Pipe	11.341			
Fire Protection Standpipe System	4.788			
Fire Pump, Electric	16.944			
Fire Protection Valve, OS&Y, 4"+	2.115			
CONVEYING				
Elevator, Cable, Electric, Passenger/Freight	95.226			
COOLING				
Chiller, Centrifugal Water Cooled, Over 100 Tons		9.886	3.598	20.440
Cooling Tower, Forced Draft, 50 to 499 Tons			4.956	4.956
Air Handling Unit, 25 to 50 Tons			1.298	0.840
Air Handling Unit, 3 to 24 Tons			6.100	4.200
Pump, Centrifugal, 1 HP +			2.392	2.392
Air Compressor, Reciprocating, 5 to 40 HP			4.856	4.856
Fan, Roof/Wall Exhaust			3.528	3.528
Fan, Axial, 36" to 48" Dia (Over 10,000 CFM)			0.695	0.695
Valve, OS&Y, 4"+				1.590
Valve, Butterfly, 4"+				0.996
Valve, Sediment Strainer, 4"+				1.252
HEATING				
Boiler, Steam, Over 1000 MBH		6.211	7.935	8.304
Pump, Centrifugal, 1 HP +			2.392	2.392
Pump, Steam Condensate Return, Duplex			5.490	
Valve, OS&Y, 4"+				0.636
Valve, Butterfly, 4"+				1.660
Valve, Sediment Strainer, 4"+				1.252
PLUMBING				
Boiler, Hot Water, 500 to 1,000 MBH		4.934	4.476	7.968
Pump, Centrifugal, 1 HP +			1.196	1.196
Pump, Storm Water, Duplex Lift			4.196	
Backflow Prevention Device, Up to 4"			0.333	
Valve, OS&Y, 4"+				0.636
ELECTRICAL				
Electrical Switchboard	0.705			
Electrical Motor Control Center		2.334		
Generator, Emergency Diesel, Over 15 kVA		3.388	2.554	10.216
Automatic Transfer Switch		0.886	0.886	3.544

Shop Labor-Hours by Frequency

	W	M	Q	S	A	Total
Fire Protection Shop Labor-Hours by Frequency =		23.424	7.388	5.865	9.561	46.238
Conveying Shop Labor-Hours by Frequency =		48.976	20.076	10.038	16.136	95.226
Cooling Shop Labor-Hours by Frequency =	11.200	9.240	12.206	17.807	32.601	83.054
Heating Shop Labor-Hours by Frequency =		8.304	5.290	7.782	14.896	36.272
Plumbing Shop Labor-Hours by Frequency =		7.968	2.984	2.688	11.295	24.935
Electric Shop Labor-Hours by Frequency =		13.760	3.440	1.720	5.593	24.513
Total Labor-Hours =	11.200	111.672	51.384	45.900	90.082	310.238

Labor-Hours per 10,000 SF = 18.2

Annualized Summary (by Level)

	Annualized Level 1	Annualized Level 2	Annualized Level 3	Annualized Level 4
Fire Protection	46.238			
Conveying	95.226			
Cooling		9.696	27.423	45.745
Heating		6.211	15.817	14.244
Plumbing		4.924	10.201	9.800
Electrical		7.313	3.440	13.760
	141.464	26.344	56.881	83.549
Labor-Hours per 10,000 SF	8.3	1.7	3.3	4.9

Compiled Labor-Hours

	Compiled Labor-Hours	Compiled Labor-Hours for 10,000 SF
Level 1	141.5	8.3
Level 1 - 2	169.8	10.0
Level 1 - 3	226.7	13.3
Level 1 - 4	310.2	18.2

GYMNASIUM BUILDING MODELS

Gymnasium Model #1: 1 Story, 20,000 SF

This model gymnasium is a concrete and masonry structure used for indoor sports such as basketball, wrestling, volleyball, indoor track, and workout equipment.

Electrical

The building's electrical systems include a 600-amp, 120/208-volt, three-phase main switch and several 120/208-volt panels for lighting and power. Lighting is supplied by a combination of incandescent, fluorescent, HID, and exit fixtures. The facility has a fire alarm annunciator system with smoke detectors and pull stations. A 60 kVA generator with an automatic transfer switch supplies power to the building's emergency systems. The facility also features intercom, data, cable television, and telephone systems.

Mechanical

The gym's mechanical systems include heating, air conditioning, ventilation, sanitary, domestic water, fire protection, and smoke removal. Cooling and heating are supplied by six 25-ton rooftop package units with gas heaters. Air distribution and ventilation are provided via metal-insulated ducts connected to the rooftop

package units and fans. An air compressor supplies control air for the pneumatic environmental control system. Localized gas hot water heaters provide domestic hot water to the restrooms and shower facilities. A wet pipe sprinkler system meets the building's fire protection requirements.

Gymnasium Model #2: Aquatic Center, 3 Stories, 120,000 SF

The Aquatic Center is a concrete and masonry structure that includes a basement. It is used for indoor sports such as basketball, competition swimming, indoor track, and volleyball.

Electrical

The electrical systems include a 3,000-amp, 277/480-volt, three-phase main switchboard; three motor control centers for equipment; and several 277/480-volt and 120/208-volt panels and dry-type transformers for lighting and power. The facility has a fire alarm annunciator system with smoke detectors and pull stations. A 200 kVA generator with an automatic transfer switch supplies power to the building's emergency systems. The facility also contains intercom, data, television, and telephone systems.

Mechanical

The mechanical systems for the aquatic center include heating, air conditioning, ventilation, sanitary, domestic water, non-potable water, fire protection, smoke removal, and elevators. The high-humidity atmosphere associated with a swimming pool requires increased maintenance of the cooling and heating equipment. Cooling is supplied by a 650-ton centrifugal chiller, a 650-ton cooling tower, a chilled water distribution system, and four 20-ton rooftop package units.

The heating system consists of an 1,800 MBH natural gas-fired steam boiler, heat exchangers, a heating hot water distribution system, and a pool hot water circulation system. Metal-insulated ducts connected to air handling units, rooftop package units, and fans provide air distribution and ventilation, and air compressors supply control air for the pneumatic environmental control system. A 1,000 MBH natural gas-fired hot water boiler provides domestic hot water to the restrooms and shower areas. Pumps circulate water between the pool and pool filters. Fire protection is addressed by a standpipe system and wet pipe sprinkler system. The facility also has a duplex lift station for removal of ground and storm water and two hydraulic elevators.

Equipment and Checklists
Sorted by System

Checklist/System Line No.	Equipment Type	Total Quantity of Each Equipment Type	Annualized Labor-Hours for Each Type of Equipment	W	M	Q	S	A	Total Annualized Labor-Hours for Each Equipment Type
FIRE PROTECTION									
PM8.2-270-1950	Fire Alarm Annunciator System	1	11.050		4.472	1.118	2.730	2.730	11.050
PM8.2-170-1950	Fire Protection System, Wet Pipe	1	11.341		3.800	2.482	1.241	3.818	11.341
PM8.2-295-1950	Fire Protection Valve, OS&Y, 4"+	2	0.423		0.352	0.088	0.044	0.362	0.846
PM8.2-275-1950	Fan, Roof Smoke Exhauster, Up to 42" x 60" & 2 HP	2	2.166		1.456	0.396	1.176	1.176	4.204
CONVEYING									
PM7.1-110-1950	Elevator, Hydraulic, Passenger/Freight	1	10.223		5.040	2.220	1.110	1.853	10.223
COOLING AND HEATING									
PM8.4-850-1950	Package/Rooftop Unit, with Duct Gas Heater	6	4.962			9.468	4.734	15.570	29.772
PM8.4-120-1950	Air Compressor, Reciprocating, Less than 5 HP	1	4.796			2.398	1.199	1.199	4.796
PM8.4-735-1950	Fan, Roof/Wall Exhaust	3	1.176				1.764	1.764	3.528
PLUMBING									
PM8.5-110-1975	Backflow Prevention Device, Up to 4", Special	1	0.666				0.333	0.333	0.666
ELECTRICAL									
PM9.3-105-2950	Generator, Emergency Diesel, Over 15 kVA	1	16.158		10.216	2.554	1.277	2.111	16.158
PM9.1-210-1950	Automatic Transfer Switch	1	5.316		3.544	0.886	0.443	0.443	5.316

Shop Labor-Hours by Frequency

Shop Labor-Hours by Frequency	W	M	Q	S	A	Total
Fire Protection Shop Labor-Hours by Frequency =		10.060	4.084	5.191	8.086	27.441
Conveying Shop Labor-Hours by Frequency =		5.040	2.220	1.110	1.853	10.223
Heating and Cooling Shop Labor-Hours by Frequency =			11.866	7.697	18.533	38.096
Plumbing Shop Labor-Hours by Frequency =				0.333	0.333	0.666
Electric Shop Labor-Hours by Frequency =		13.760	3.440	1.720	2.554	21.474
Total Labor-Hours =		28.880	21.610	16.051	31.359	97.900

Labor-Hours per 10,000 SF = 48.9

Level Distribution

Equipment Type	Level 1 Labor-Hours	Level 2 Labor-Hours	Level 3 Labor-Hours	Level 4 Labor-Hours
FIRE PROTECTION				
Fire Alarm Annunciator System	11.050			
Fire Protection System, Wet Pipe	11.341			
Fire Protection Valve, OS&Y, 4"+	0.846			
Fan, Roof Smoke Exhauster	4.204			
CONVEYING				
Elevator, Hydraulic, Passenger/Freight	10.223			
COOLING AND HEATING				
Package/Rooftop Unit			15.570	14.202
Air Compressor			2.398	2.398
Fan, Roof/Wall Exhaust			1.764	1.764
PLUMBING				
Backflow Prevention Device			0.333	0.333
ELECTRICAL				
Generator, Emergency Diesel		3.388	2.554	10.216
Automatic Transfer Switch		0.886	0.886	3.544

	Level 1 Annualized	Level 2 Annualized	Level 3 Annualized	Level 4 Annualized
	27.441		19.732	18.364
	10.223		0.333	0.333
		4.274	3.440	13.760
		4.274	23.505	32.457
	37.664	2.1	11.8	16.2
	18.8	20.9	32.7	48.9
		41.936	65.443	97.900

Compiled Labor-Hours:
- Level 1 = 37.664
- Level 1 - 2 = 41.936
- Level 1 - 3 = 65.443
- Level 1 - 4 = 97.900

Compiled Labor-Hours for 10,000 SF:
- Level 1 = 18.8
- Level 1 - 2 = 20.9
- Level 1 - 3 = 32.7
- Level 1 - 4 = 48.9

GYMNASIUM MODEL NO. 1
1 STORY, 20,000 SF

GYMNASIUM MODEL NO. 2
3 STORIES, 120,000 SF

Equipment and Checklists — Sorted by System

Checklist/System Line No.	Equipment Type	Total Quantity of Each Equipment Type	Annualized Labor-Hours for Each Type of Equipment	W	M	Q	S	A	Total Annualized Labor-Hours for Each Equipment Type
FIRE PROTECTION									
PM8.2-270-1950	Fire Alarm Annunciator System	1	11.050		4.472	2.730	1.118	2.730	11.050
PM8.2-170-1950	Fire Protection System, Wet Pipe	1	11.341		3.850	1.241	2.482	3.818	11.341
PM8.2-180-1950	Fire Protection Standpipe System	1	4.788		2.976	0.744	0.372	0.696	4.788
PM8.2-250-1950	Fire Pump, Electric	1	16.944		11.236	2.824	1.412	1.412	16.944
PM8.2-295-1950	Fire Protection Valve, OS&Y, 4"+	5	0.423		0.880	0.220	0.110	0.905	2.115
CONVEYING									
PM7.1-110-1950	Elevator, Hydraulic, Passenger/Freight	2	10.223						20.446
COOLING									
PM8.4-220-2950	Chiller, Centrifugal Water Cooled, Over 100 Tons	1	33.924	11.200	9.240	2.310	1.288	9.886	33.924
PM8.4-510-2950	Cooling Tower, Forced Draft, 50 to 499 Tons	1	9.912		4.956			4.956	9.912
PM8.4-160-2975	Air Handling Unit, 25 to 50 Tons, Special	4	3.746		6.432	3.360	1.680	3.512	14.984
PM8.4-160-1950	Air Handling Unit, 3 to 24 Tons, Special	4	3.668		5.898	3.360	1.680	3.200	14.138
PM8.4-810-1950	Package/Rooftop Unit, 3 to 24 Tons	2	2.402		1.864	0.932		2.008	4.804
PM8.4-015-1950	Pump, Centrifugal, 1 HP+	4	1.196		2.392			2.392	4.784
PM8.4-120-2950	Pump, Centrifugal, 1 HP+	4	1.196		2.392			2.392	4.804
PM8.4-735-1950	Air Compressor, Reciprocating, 5 to 40 HP	2	4.856		2.428	2.428		4.856	9.712
PM8.4-710-3975	Fan, Roof/Wall Exhaust	6	1.176		3.528			3.528	7.056
PM8.4-710-3975	Fan, Axial, 36 to 48 Dia (Over 10,000 CFM), Special	4	1.522		2.844	0.400		2.844	6.088
PM8.5-355-1950	Valve, OS&Y, 4"+	4	0.159					0.636	0.636
PM8.5-320-1950	Valve, Butterfly, 4"+	10	0.166					1.660	1.660
PM8.5-350-1950	Valve, Motor Operated, 4"+	4	1.002		2.004			2.004	4.008
PM8.5-370-1950	Valve, Sediment Strainer, 4"+	4	0.313					1.252	1.252
HEATING									
PM8.3-160-4975	Boiler, Steam, Over 1,000 MBH, Special	1	35.842	11.800	9.896	5.290	2.845		35.842
PM8.4-015-1950	Pump, Centrifugal, 1 HP+	12	1.196		7.176			7.176	14.352
PM8.3-710-3950	Pump, Steam Condensate Return, Duplex	2	1.098		1.098			1.098	2.196
PM8.5-355-1950	Valve, OS&Y, 4"+	18	0.159					2.862	2.862
PM8.5-320-1950	Valve, Butterfly, 4"+	7	0.166					1.162	1.162
PM8.5-350-1950	Valve, Motor Operated, 4"+	4	1.002		2.004			2.004	4.008
PM8.5-370-1950	Valve, Sediment Strainer, 4"+	12	0.313					3.756	3.756
PLUMBING									
PM8.5-170-2950	Pump, Split-Case	4	2.392		2.356		4.784	2.356	9.496
PM8.4-015-1950	Pump, Centrifugal, 1 HP+	12	1.196		7.176			7.176	14.352
PM8.3-120-3950	Boiler, Hot Water, 500 to 1,000 MBH	1	17.378		7.968	2.984	1.492	4.934	17.378
PM8.4-015-1950	Pump, Centrifugal, 1 HP+	4	1.196		2.392			2.392	4.784
PM8.4-020-2950	Pump, Storm Water, Duplex Lift	4	1.049					4.196	4.196
PM8.5-355-1950	Valve, OS&Y, 4"+	4	0.159					0.636	0.636
PM8.5-320-1950	Valve, Butterfly, 4"+	33	0.166					5.478	5.478
PM8.5-340-1950	Valve, Gate, 4"+	1	0.159					0.159	0.159
PM8.5-110-2975	Backflow Preventer, 4"+, Special	2	0.988				0.988	0.988	1.976
ELECTRICAL									
PM9.1-150-1950	Electrical Switchboard	1	0.705					0.705	0.705
PM9.2-110-1950	Electrical Motor Control Center	3	0.389					1.167	1.167
PM9.3-105-2950	Generator, Emergency Diesel, Over 15 kVA	1	16.158		10.216	2.554			16.158
PM9.1-210-1950	Automatic Transfer Switch	1	5.316					5.316	5.316

Shop Labor-Hours by Frequency

	W	M	Q	S	A	
Fire Protection Shop Labor-Hours by Frequency =		23.424	10.080	5.865	9.561	46.238
Conveying Shop Labor-Hours by Frequency =		11.200?	21.570	4.440	2.220	20.446
Cooling Shop Labor-Hours by Frequency =	11.200	21.570	23.732	16.150	40.306	112.958
Heating Shop Labor-Hours by Frequency =	11.800	9.896	12.923	24.269	40.743	64.178
Plumbing Shop Labor-Hours by Frequency =		13.760	7.968	5.340	14.404	58.455
Electric Shop Labor-Hours by Frequency =		7.968	3.440	1.720	4.426	23.346
Total Labor-Hours =	23.000	86.698	42.048	60.864	113.011	325.621
Labor-Hours per 10,000 SF =						27.2

Compiled Labor-Hours

	Compiled Labor-Hours	Compiled Labor-Hours for 10,000 SF
Level 1	66.7	5.6
Level 1 - 2	105.8	8.9
Level 1 - 3	181.3	15.2
Level 1 - 4	325.6	27.2

Total Annualized Labor-Hours for Each Equipment Type (Annualized by System)

System	Level 1	Level 2	Level 3	Level 4	Annualized
FIRE PROTECTION	11.050	11.341	4.788	16.944 / 2.115	46.238
CONVEYING	20.446				20.446
COOLING	33.924 / 9.912				112.958
HEATING	35.842	6.211			64.178
PLUMBING	9.496	7.176			58.455
ELECTRICAL	0.705	1.167			23.346

LABORATORY BUILDING MODELS

Laboratory Model #1: 1-2 Stories, 45,000 SF

This model laboratory is a two-story, concrete and masonry structure used for science or research laboratories. The building's systems allow for heavy-duty, production-type activities related to experiments or testing.

Electrical

The electrical systems include a 2,000 amp, 277/480-volt, three-phase main switchboard; a motor control center; and several 277/480-volt and 120/208-volt panels for lighting and power. Incandescent, fluorescent, HID, and exit fixtures are used for lighting. The facility has a fire alarm annunciator system with smoke detectors and pull stations. Emergency power is available through a 60 kVA generator with an automatic transfer switch. The building also contains intercom, data, cable television, and telephone systems.

Mechanical

The mechanical systems include heating, air conditioning, ventilation, sanitary, natural gas, domestic water, fire protection, and an elevator. Cooling and heating are supplied by six 25-ton rooftop package units with gas heaters. Air distribution and ventilation are provided via metal-insulated ducts connected to the rooftop package units, fume hoods, and fans. An air compressor supplies control air for the pneumatic environmental control system. A 500 MBH natural gas-fired hot water boiler supplies domestic hot water to the restrooms and laboratory work stations. The fire protection for the building is from a wet pipe sprinkler system. A hydraulic elevator provides service between the first and second floors.

Laboratory Model #2: 3-4 Stories, 100,000 SF

This larger laboratory facility is a four-story, concrete and masonry structure that houses heavy-duty production-type experiments or testing.

Electrical

The building's electrical systems include a 4,000-amp, 277/480-volt, three-phase main switchboard; five motor control centers; and various 277/480-volt and 120/208-volt panels for lighting and power. The facility has a fire alarm annunciator system with smoke detectors and pull stations. Emergency power is delivered by a 150 kVA generator with an associated automatic transfer switch. The building also contains intercom, data, cable television, and telephone systems.

Mechanical

The mechanical systems include heating, air conditioning, ventilation, sanitary, natural gas, domestic water, fire protection, and elevators. Cooling is supplied by four 50-ton, water-cooled reciprocating chillers, a 200-ton cooling tower, a 25-ton, air-cooled reciprocating chiller, and a chilled water distribution system. The heating system consists of a 1,000 MBH natural gas-fired steam boiler, heat exchangers, and a heating hot water distribution system.

Air distribution and ventilation is via metal-insulated ducts connected to air handling units, fume hoods, and fans. An air compressor supplies control air for the pneumatic environmental control system. A 750 MBH natural gas-fired hot water boiler supplies domestic hot water. The facility also has a duplex lift station for removal of ground and storm water. Fire protection consists of a standpipe and wet pipe sprinkler system. Two hydraulic elevators provide service between the first and fourth floors.

Equipment and Checklists — Sorted by System

Checklist/System Line No.	Equipment Type	Total Quantity of Each Equipment Type	Annualized Labor-Hours for Each Type of Equipment	W	M	Q	S	A	Total Annualized Labor-Hours for Each Equipment Type
FIRE PROTECTION									
PM8.2-270-1950	Fire Alarm Annunciator System	1	11.050		4.472	1.118	2.730	2.730	11.050
PM8.2-170-1950	Fire Protection System, Wet Pipe	1	11.341		3.800	2.482	1.241	3.818	11.341
PM8.2-295-1950	Fire Protection Valve, OS&Y, 4"+	2	0.423		0.352	0.088	0.044	0.362	0.846
CONVEYING									
PM7.1-110-1950	Elevator, Hydraulic, Passenger/Freight	1	10.223		5.040	2.220	1.110	1.853	10.223
COOLING AND HEATING									
PM8.4-850-1950	Package/Rooftop Unit, with Duct Gas Heater	6	4.962			9.468	4.734	15.570	29.772
PM8.4-120-1950	Air Compressor, Reciprocating, Less than 5 HP	1	4.796			2.398	1.199	1.199	4.796
PM8.4-740-1950	Fan, Fume Hood, Utility Exhaust	25	4.840		75.200	18.800	13.500	3.246	110.740
PM8.4-735-1950	Fan, Roof/Wall Exhaust	6	1.176				3.528	3.528	7.056
PLUMBING									
PM8.5-110-1975	Backflow Prevention Device, Up To 4", Special	1	0.666				0.333	0.333	0.666
PM8.3-120-2950	Boiler, Hot Water, 120 to 500 MBH	1	15.448		7.272	2.720	1.360	4.096	15.448
ELECTRICAL									
PM9.1-150-1950	Switchboard, Electrical	1	0.705					0.705	0.705
PM9.2-110-1950	Motor Control Center, Electric	1	0.389					0.389	0.389
PM9.3-105-2950	Generator, Emergency Diesel, Over 15 kVA	1	16.158		10.216	2.554	1.277	2.111	16.158
PM9.1-210-1950	Automatic Transfer Switch	1	5.316		3.544	0.886	0.443	0.443	5.316

(Labor-Hours by PM Frequencies for Total Quantities of Equipment: W, M, Q, S, A)

Level Labor-Hours

Equipment Type	Level 1	Level 2	Level 3	Level 4
FIRE PROTECTION				
Fire Alarm Annunciator System	11.050			
Fire Protection System, Wet Pipe	11.341			
Fire Protection Valve, OS&Y, 4"+	0.846			
CONVEYING				
Elevator, Hydraulic, Passenger/Freight	10.223			
COOLING AND HEATING				
Package/Rooftop Unit			15.570	14.202
Air Compressor			2.398	2.398
Fan, Fume Hood, Utility Exhaust		3.240	32.300	75.200
Fan, Roof/Wall Exhaust			3.528	3.528
PLUMBING				
Backflow Prevention Device			0.333	0.333
Boiler, Hot Water		4.096	4.090	7.272
ELECTRICAL				
Switchboard, Electrical		0.706		
Motor Control Center		0.389		
Generator, Emergency Diesel		3.388	2.554	10.216
Automatic Transfer Switch		0.886	0.886	3.544

Shop Labor-Hours by Frequency

Shop	W	M	Q	S	A	Annualized
Fire Protection Shop Labor-Hours by Frequency =		8.624	3.688	4.015	6.910	23.237
Conveying Shop Labor-Hours by Frequency =		5.040	2.220	1.110	1.853	10.223
Heating and Cooling Shop Labor-Hours by Frequency =		75.200	30.666	22.961	23.537	152.364
Plumbing Shop Labor-Hours by Frequency =		7.272	2.720	1.693	4.429	16.114
Electric Shop Labor-Hours by Frequency =		13.760	3.440	1.720	3.648	22.568
Total Labor-Hours =		109.896	42.734	31.499	40.377	224.506

Labor-Hours per 10,000 SF = 49.8

Shop Annualized Labor-Hours by Level

Shop	Level 1	Level 2	Level 3	Level 4
Fire Protection	23.237			
Conveying	10.223			
Heating and Cooling		3.240	53.796	95.328
Plumbing		4.036	4.413	7.605
Electric		5.368	3.440	13.760
Total	33.460	12.704	61.649	116.693
per 10,000 SF	7.4	2.8	13.7	25.9

Compiled Labor-Hours

	Compiled Labor-Hours	Compiled Labor-Hours for 10,000 SF
Level 1	33.460	7.4
Level 1 - 2	46.164	10.2
Level 1 - 3	107.813	23.9
Level 1 - 4	224.506	49.8

LABORATORY MODEL NO. 1
1-2 STORIES, 45,000 SF

LABORATORY MODEL NO. 2 — 3-4 STORIES, 100,000 SF

Equipment and Checklists
Sorted by System

Checklist/System Line No.	Equipment Type	Total Quantity of Each Type of Equipment	Annualized Labor-Hours for Each Type of Equipment	W	M	Q	S	A	Total Annualized Labor-Hours for Each Equipment Type
FIRE PROTECTION									
PM8.2-270-1950	Fire Alarm Annunciator System	1	11.050	4.472	1.116		2.730	2.730	11.050
PM8.2-170-1950	Fire Protection System, Wet Pipe	1	11.341	3.800	2.482	1.241		3.818	11.341
PM8.2-180-1950	Fire Protection Standpipe System	1	4.788	2.976	0.744	0.372		0.696	4.788
PM8.2-260-1950	Fire Pump, Electric	1	16.944	11.296	2.824	1.412		1.412	16.944
PM8.2-295-1950	Fire Protection Valve, OS&Y, 4"+	5	0.423	0.880	0.220	0.110		0.905	2.115
CONVEYING									
PM7.1-110-1950	Elevator, Hydraulic, Passenger/Freight	2	10.223	10.080	4.440	2.220	3.706	3.706	20.446
COOLING									
PM8.4-230-2950	Chiller, Recip. Air Cooled 25 Tons +	1	12.887	6.992	1.748	0.874	3.237	3.237	12.887
PM8.4-240-2950	Chiller, Recip. Water Cooled, 50 Tons +	4	10.907	27.968	6.992	3.496	5.172	5.172	43.628
PM8.4-510-2950	Cooling Tower, Forced Draft, 50 to 499 Tons	1	9.912	9.912	4.956	4.956	4.956	4.956	9.912
PM8.4-160-2975	Air Handling Unit, 25 to 50 Tons, Special	4	3.746	9.792					14.984
PM8.4-160-1975	Air Handling Unit, 3 to 24 Tons, Special	3		8.416	3.360	1.680	2.400	3.512	12.078
PM8.4-015-1950	Pump, Centrifugal, 1 HP +	8	1.196	3.668	2.520	1.260	4.784	4.784	9.568
PM8.4-120-2950	Air Compressor, Reciprocating, 5 to 40 HP	3	4.856	7.284	7.284	3.642	4.784	4.784	14.568
PM8.4-735-1950	Fan, Roof/Wall Exhaust	6	1.176	3.528		3.528	3.528	3.528	7.056
PM8.4-710-3975	Fan, Axial, 36" to 48" Dia (Over 10,000 CFM), Special	4	1.522	2.844	1.522	2.844	2.844	2.844	6.088
PM8.4-740-1950	Fan, Fume Hood, Utility Exhaust	50	4.840	150.400	97.600	27.000	10.800	10.800	225.800
PM8.4-335-1950	Valve, OS&Y, 4"+	20	0.159	3.180		3.180	3.180	3.180	3.180
PM8.4-320-1950	Valve, Butterfly, 4"+	8	0.166	1.328			1.328	1.328	1.328
PM8.5-350-1950	Valve, Motor Operated, 4"+	6	1.002	6.012	7.284	3.006	3.006	6.012	6.012
PM8.5-370-1950	Valve, Sediment Strainer, 4"+	8	0.313	0.313			3.006	2.504	2.504
HEATING									
PM8.3-160-4950	Boiler, Steam, Over 1000 MBH	1	22.450	8.304	5.290	2.645	6.211	6.211	22.450
PM8.4-015-1950	Pump, Centrifugal, 1 HP +	8	1.196	1.196		4.784	4.784	4.784	9.568
PM8.3-710-3950	Pump, Steam Condensate Return, Duplex	2	1.142	1.142		1.098	1.098	1.098	2.196
PM8.5-335-1950	Valve, OS&Y, 4"+	20	0.159	0.159		3.180	3.180	3.180	3.180
PM8.5-320-1950	Valve, Butterfly, 4"+	8	0.166	0.166			1.328	1.328	1.328
PM8.5-350-1950	Valve, Motor Operated, 4"+	6	1.002	1.002			3.006	6.012	6.012
PM8.5-370-1950	Valve, Sediment Strainer, 4"+	8	0.313	0.313			3.006	2.504	2.504
PLUMBING									
PM8.3-120-3950	Boiler, Hot Water, 500 to 1,000 MBH	1	17.378	7.968	2.984	1.492	4.934	4.934	17.378
PM8.4-015-1950	Pump, Centrifugal, 1 HP +	2	1.196		1.196	1.196	1.196	1.196	2.392
PM8.4-020-2950	Pump, Storm Water, Duplex Lift	1	4.196		4.196				4.196
PM8.5-110-2975	Backflow Prevention Device, Up to 4", Special	1	0.666		0.666		0.333	0.333	0.666
PM8.5-355-1950	Valve, OS&Y, 4"+	6	0.159				0.954	0.954	0.954
ELECTRICAL									
PM9.1-150-1950	Electrical Switchboard	1	0.705				0.705	0.705	0.705
PM9.2-110-1950	Electrical Motor Control Center	5	0.389				1.945	1.945	1.945
PM9.3-105-2950	Generator, Emergency Diesel, Over 15 kVA	1	16.158	16.158	10.216	2.554	2.111	2.111	16.158
PM9.1-210-1950	Automatic Transfer Switch	1	5.316	5.316	3.544	0.886	0.443	0.443	5.316

Shop Labor-Hours by Frequency

	W	M	Q	S	A	Compiled Labor-Hours
Fire Protection Shop Labor-Hours by Frequency =	23.424	10.080	7.388	5.865	9.561	46.238
Conveying Shop Labor-Hours by Frequency =	10.080	4.440	2.220	3.706	3.706	20.446
Cooling Shop Labor-Hours by Frequency =	197.690	59.904	57.070	54.893	54.893	369.557
Heating Shop Labor-Hours by Frequency =	8.304	5.290	11.533	22.111	22.111	47.238
Plumbing Shop Labor-Hours by Frequency =	7.968	2.984	3.021	11.613	11.613	25.586
Electric Shop Labor-Hours by Frequency =	13.760	3.440	1.720	5.204	5.204	24.124
Total Labor-Hours by Frequency =	261.226	83.446	107.088	81.429	107.088	533.189

Compiled Labor-Hours = 533.189
Labor-Hours per 10,000 SF = 53.4

Total Annualized Labor-Hours for Each Equipment Type (by Level)

	Level 1 Labor-Hours	Level 2 Labor-Hours	Level 3 Labor-Hours	Level 4 Labor-Hours
FIRE PROTECTION				
	11.050			
	11.341			
	4.788			
	16.944			
	2.115			
CONVEYING				
	20.446			
COOLING				
	1.748	4.111	6.992	6.992
	6.992	8.668	27.968	27.968
	4.956		4.956	4.956
	5.192		9.792	9.792
	3.660		3.660	8.416
	1.260		6.211	14.915
	4.784		4.934	10.201
	3.642		5.924	13.760
	3.528		3.440	3.440
	2.844		41.648	134.144
	27.000	64.600	105.588	225.800
	3.180		3.388	3.244
	1.328		2.554	2.844
	6.012			6.012
	2.504			2.504
HEATING				
	6.211	7.935	22.450	22.450
	4.784		4.784	26.112
	2.196		2.196	10.451
	3.180			13.760
	1.328			3.440
	6.012			
	2.504			
PLUMBING				
	4.934	4.476	17.378	240.390
	1.196	1.196	1.196	
	4.196	2.554	4.196	
	0.333	0.333	0.333	
	0.954			
ELECTRICAL				
	0.705	0.705	0.705	
	1.945	1.945	1.945	
	16.158	3.388	2.554	10.216
	5.316	0.886	0.886	3.544

	Annualized	Annualized	Annualized	Annualized
FIRE PROTECTION	46.238			
	20.446			
CONVEYING	20.446			
COOLING			105.588	290.713
HEATING				29.1
PLUMBING	66.604	41.648	134.144	
ELECTRICAL	4.2		13.4	

	Compiled Labor-Hours =	Labor-Hours for 10,000 SF =
Level 1	66.7	6.7
Level 1 - 2	108.3	10.9
Level 1 - 3	242.5	24.3
Level 1 - 4	533.2	53.4

LIBRARY BUILDING MODELS

Library Model #1: 1-4 Stories, 60,000 SF

This model library is a four-story, concrete and masonry structure that would typically be open 24 hours a day, 7 days a week. The building includes a rare book section with separate temperature and humidity controls.

Electrical

This facility's electrical systems include a 1,600-amp, 120/208-volt, three-phase main switchboard; motor control centers for equipment; and panels for lighting and power. Lighting fixtures are a combination of incandescent, fluorescent, HID, and exit lights. The facility has a fire alarm annunciator system with smoke detectors and pull stations. A 60 kVA generator supplies power to emergency systems throughout the building. Other electrical systems include intercom, data, cable television, and telephones.

Mechanical

Mechanical systems include heating, air conditioning, ventilation, sanitary, domestic water, and elevators. Cooling is supplied by a 150-ton centrifugal chiller, a 150-ton cooling tower, and a chilled water distribution system. A 25-ton rooftop package unit services the rare book section. Heating is supplied by a 1,000 MBH natural

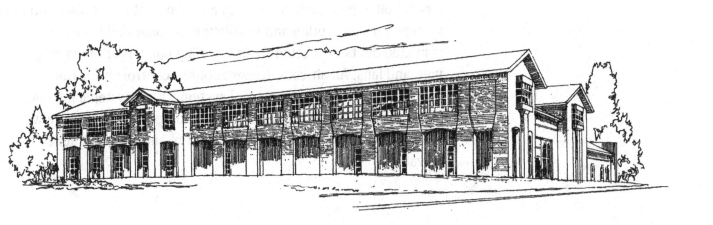

gas-fired hot water boiler and a heating hot water distribution system. Air distribution and ventilation is via metal-insulated ducts connected to air handling units, a rooftop package unit, and fans. An air compressor supplies control air for the pneumatic environmental control system. Localized electric hot water heaters provide domestic hot water to the restrooms and lounges. Standpipe and wet pipe sprinkler systems provide fire protection. The facility also has a duplex lift station for removal of ground and storm water. There are two hydraulic elevators.

Library Model #2: 4-5 Stories, 400,000 SF

This larger library model is a five-story, concrete and masonry structure. The building would generally be open 24 hours a day, 7 days a week, and contains a rare book/valuable document section with independent temperature and humidity controls.

Electrical

This building's electrical systems include a 3,000-amp, 277/480-volt, three-phase main switchboard; six motor control centers for controlling equipment; and several 277/480-volt and 120/208-volt panels for lighting and power. Lighting is a combination of incandescent, fluorescent, HID, and exit fixtures. The facility has a fire alarm annunciator system with smoke detectors and pull stations. A 150 kVA generator with an automatic transfer switch supplies power to the building's emergency systems. Other systems include intercom, data, cable television, and telephone.

Mechanical

The mechanical systems include heating, air conditioning, ventilation, sanitary, domestic water, fire protection, and four elevators. Cooling is supplied by a 650-ton centrifugal chiller, a 650-ton cooling tower, a chilled water distribution system, and a 25-ton rooftop package unit that specifically services the rare book section. Heating is supplied by an 1,800 MBH natural gas-fired steam boiler, heat exchangers, and a heating hot water distribution system. Air distribution and ventilation are provided via metal-insulated ducts connected to air handling units, rooftop package unit, and fans. An air compressor supplies control air for the pneumatic environmental control system. Other systems include localized electric hot water heaters, a standpipe system and a wet pipe sprinkler system, a duplex lift station, and four hydraulic elevators.

Equipment and Checklists — Sorted by System

Checklist/System Line No.	Equipment Type	Total Quantity of Each Equipment Type	Annualized Labor-Hours for Each Type of Equipment	W	M	Q	S	A	Total Annualized Labor-Hours for Each Equipment Type	Level 1 Labor-Hours	Level 2 Labor-Hours	Level 3 Labor-Hours	Level 4 Labor-Hours
FIRE PROTECTION													
PM8.2-270-1950	Fire Alarm Annunciator System	1	11.050		4.472	1.118	2.730	2.730	11.050	11.050			
PM8.2-170-1950	Fire Protection System, Wet Pipe	1	11.341		3.800	2.482	1.241	3.818	11.341	11.341			
PM8.2-180-1950	Fire Protection Standpipe System	1	4.788		2.976	0.744	0.372	0.696	4.788	4.788			
PM8.2-296-1950	Fire Protection Valve, OS&Y, 4"+	3	0.423		0.528	0.132	0.066	0.543	1.269	1.269			
CONVEYING													
PM7.1-110-1950	Elevator, Hydraulic, Passenger/Freight	2	10.223		10.080	4.440	2.220	3.706	20.446	20.446			
COOLING													
PM8.4-220-2950	Chiller, Centrifugal Water Cooled, Over 100 Tons	1	33.924	11.200	9.240	2.310	1.283	9.886	33.924		9.886	3.598	20.440
PM8.4-510-2950	Cooling Tower, Forced Draft, 50 to 499 Tons	1	9.912				4.956	4.956	9.912			4.956	4.956
PM8.4-160-1950	Air Handling Unit, 3 to 24 Tons	6	2.060			5.040	2.520	4.800	12.360			7.320	5.040
PM8.4-810-1950	Package/Rooftop Unit, 3 to 24 Tons	1	2.402			0.932	0.466	1.004	2.402			1.004	1.398
PM8.4-015-1950	Pump, Centrifugal, 1 HP +	6	1.196				3.588	3.588	7.176			3.588	3.588
PM8.4-120-1950	Air Compressor, Reciprocating, Less than 5 HP	1	4.796			2.398	1.199	1.199	4.796			2.398	2.398
PM8.4-735-1950	Fan, Roof/Wall Exhaust	8	1.176				4.704	4.704	9.408			4.704	4.704
PM8.5-355-1950	Valve, OS&Y, 4"+	12	0.159					1.908	1.908				1.908
PM8.5-320-1950	Valve, Butterfly, 4"+	6	0.166					0.996	0.996				0.996
PM8.5-350-1950	Valve, Motor Operated, 4"+	6	1.002				3.006	3.006	6.012				6.012
PM8.5-370-1950	Valve, Sediment Strainer, 4"+	6	0.313					1.878	1.878				1.878
HEATING													
PM8.3-120-4950	Boiler, Hot Water, Over 1,000 MBH	1	19.698		9.352	3.418	1.709	5.219	19.698		5.219	5.127	9.352
PM8.4-015-1950	Pump, Centrifugal, 1 HP +	6	1.196				3.588	3.588	7.176			3.588	3.588
PM8.5-355-1950	Valve, OS&Y, 4"+	6	0.159					0.954	0.954				0.954
PM8.5-320-1950	Valve, Butterfly, 4"+	6	0.166					0.996	0.996				0.996
PM8.5-350-1950	Valve, Motor Operated, 4"+	6	1.002				3.006	3.006	6.012				6.012
PM8.5-370-1950	Valve, Sediment Strainer, 4"+	6	0.313					1.878	1.878				1.878
PLUMBING													
PM8.4-020-2950	Pump, Storm Water, Duplex Lift	1	4.196					4.196	4.196			4.196	
PM8.5-110-1950	Backflow Prevention Device, Up to 4"	1	0.333					0.333	0.333			0.333	
PM8.5-340-1950	Valve, Gate, 4"	2	0.159					0.318	0.318		0.318		
ELECTRICAL													
PM9.1-150-1950	Electrical Switchboard	1	0.705					0.705	0.705		0.705		
PM9.2-110-1950	Electrical Motor Control Center	3	0.389					1.167	1.167		1.167		
PM9.3-105-2950	Generator, Emergency Diesel, Over 15 kVA	1	16.158		10.216	2.554	1.277	2.111	16.158		3.388	2.554	10.216
PM9.1-210-1950	Automatic Transfer Switch	1	5.316		3.544	0.886	0.443	0.443	5.316		0.886	0.686	3.544

Shop Labor-Hours by Frequency

	W	M	Q	S	A	Annualized
Fire Protection Shop Labor-Hours by Frequency =		11.776	4.476	4.409	7.787	28.448
Conveying Shop Labor-Hours by Frequency =		10.080	4.440	2.220	3.706	20.446
Cooling Shop Labor-Hours by Frequency =	11.200	9.240	10.680	21.727	37.925	90.772
Heating Shop Labor-Hours by Frequency =		9.352	3.418	8.303	15.641	36.714
Plumbing Shop Labor-Hours by Frequency =				1.720	4.847	4.847
Electric Shop Labor-Hours by Frequency =		13.760	3.440	1.720	4.426	23.346
Total I Labor-Hours =	11.200	54.208	26.454	38.379	74.332	204.573

Labor-Hours per 10,000 SF = 34.0

Compiled Labor-Hours

Level 1	= 48.9
Level 1 - 2	= 70.1
Level 1 - 3	= 114.4
Level 1 - 4	= 204.6

Compiled Labor-Hours for 10,000 SF

Level 1	= 8.1
Level 1 - 2	= 11.6
Level 1 - 3	= 19.0
Level 1 - 4	= 34.0

LIBRARY MODEL NO. 1
1-4 STORIES, 60,000 SF

LIBRARY MODEL NO. 2 — 4-5 STORIES, 400,000 SF

Equipment and Checklists
Sorted by System

Legend of frequency columns: W = Weekly, M = Monthly, Q = Quarterly, S = Semi-Annual, A = Annual. The W/M/Q/S/A columns give "Labor-Hours by PM Frequencies for Total Quantities of Equipment." (Only clearly legible frequency cells are filled below.)

Checklist/System Line No.	Equipment Type	Total Qty of Each Equipment Type	Annualized Labor-Hours for Each Type of Equipment	W	M	Q	S	A	Total Annualized Labor-Hours for Each Equipment Type
FIRE PROTECTION									
PM8.2-270-1950	Fire Alarm Annunciator System	1	11.050		4.472	1.118	2.730	2.730	11.050
PM8.2-170-1950	Fire Protection System, Wet Pipe	1	11.341		3.800	2.482	1.241	3.818	11.341
PM8.2-180-1950	Fire Protection Standpipe System	1	4.788		2.976	0.744	0.372	0.696	4.788
PM8.2-250-1950	Fire Pump, Electric	1	16.944		11.296	2.824	1.412	1.412	16.944
PM8.2-295-1950	Fire Protection Valve, OS&Y, 4"+	5	0.423		0.880	0.220	0.110	0.905	2.115
CONVEYING									
PM7.1-110-1950	Elevator, Hydraulic, Passenger/Freight	4	10.223		20.160	8.880	4.440	7.412	40.892
COOLING									
PM8.4-220-2950	Chiller, Centrifugal Water Cooled, Over 100 Tons	1	33.924	11.200	9.240	3.588		9.896	33.924
PM8.4-510-3950	Cooling Tower, Forced Draft, 500 to 1000 Tons	1	17.728					8.864	17.728
PM8.4-160-2950	Air Handling Unit, 25 to 50 Tons	5	2.138					4.390	10.690
PM8.4-160-1950	Air Handling Unit, 3 to 24 Tons	8	2.060					6.400	16.480
PM8.4-810-1950	Package/Rooftop Unit, 3 to 24 Tons	1	2.402					1.004	2.402
PM8.4-015-1950	Pump, Centrifugal, 1 HP +	10	1.196					5.980	11.960
PM8.4-120-2950	Air Compressor, Reciprocating, 5 to 40 HP	2	4.856					2.428	9.712
PM8.4-735-1950	Fan, Roof/Wall Exhaust	20	1.176					11.760	23.520
PM8.4-710-3950	Fan, Axial, 36" to 48" Dia (Over 10,000 CFM)	5	1.390					3.475	6.950
PM8.5-355-1950	Valve, OS&Y, 4"+	16	0.159					2.544	2.544
PM8.5-320-1950	Valve, Butterfly, 4"	5	0.166					0.830	0.830
PM8.5-340-1950	Valve, Gate, 4"	3	0.159					0.477	0.477
PM8.5-350-1950	Valve, Motor Operated, 4"	5	1.002				2.505	2.505	5.010
PM8.5-370-1950	Valve, Sediment Strainer, 4"	10	0.313					3.130	3.130
HEATING									
PM8.3-160-4950	Boiler, Steam, Over 1,000 MBH	1	22.450						22.450
PM8.4-015-1950	Pump, Centrifugal, 1 HP +	8	1.196						9.568
PM8.4-710-3950	Pump, Steam Condensate Return, Duplex	5	1.142						5.490
PM8.5-355-1950	Valve, OS&Y, 4"+	16	0.159					2.544	2.544
PM8.5-320-1950	Valve, Butterfly, 4"	5	0.166					0.830	0.830
PM8.5-350-1950	Valve, Motor Operated, 4"	5	1.002				2.505	2.505	5.010
PM8.5-370-1950	Valve, Sediment Strainer, 4"	10	0.313					3.130	3.130
PLUMBING									
PM8.4-020-2950	Pump, Storm Water, Duplex Lift	1	4.196						4.196
PM8.5-340-1950	Valve, Gate, 4"	8	0.159					1.272	1.272
PM8.5-110-1950	Backflow Prevention Device, Up to 4"	1	0.333						0.333
PM8.5-355-1950	Valve, OS&Y, 4" +	4	0.159					0.636	0.636
ELECTRICAL									
PM9.1-150-1950	Electrical Switchboard	1	0.705					0.705	0.705
PM9.2-110-1950	Electrical Motor Control Center	6	0.389					2.334	2.334
PM9.3-105-2950	Generator, Emergency Diesel, Over 15 kVA	1	16.158						16.158
PM9.1-210-1950	Automatic Transfer Switch	1	5.316						5.316

Total Annualized Labor-Hours by System

System	Annualized
FIRE PROTECTION	46.238
CONVEYING	40.892
COOLING	145.357
HEATING	48.396
PLUMBING	6.437
ELECTRICAL	24.513

Shop Labor-Hours by Frequency

System	W	M	Q	S	A	Total
Fire Protection Shop Labor-Hours by Frequency =		23.424	7.388	5.865	9.561	46.238
Conveying Shop Labor-Hours by Frequency =		20.160	8.880	4.440	7.412	40.892
Cooling Shop Labor-Hours by Frequency =	11.200	9.240	19.018	42.226	63.673	145.357
Heating Shop Labor-Hours by Frequency =						48.396
Plumbing Shop Labor-Hours by Frequency =						6.437
Electric Shop Labor-Hours by Frequency =						24.513
Total Labor-Hours =	11.200					311.833

Compiled Labor-Hours

	Compiled Labor-Hours	Compiled Labor-Hours for 10,000 SF
Level 1	87.130	2.2
Level 1 - 2	110.5	2.8
Level 1 - 3	192.5	4.8
Level 1 - 4	311.833	7.8

Labor-Hours per 10,000 SF = 7.8

PERFORMING ARTS BUILDING MODEL

Performing Arts Center: 1-2 Stories, 50,000 SF

The model Performing Arts Center is a two-story, concrete and masonry structure used as a theater and auditorium. There are many pieces of performance-related specialty equipment in this facility, such as stage lifts, theater curtains, and lighting and sound systems. These items are the responsibility of the building manager and are maintained by specialty staff or contractors. Therefore, they have not been included in this PM program.

Electrical

The electrical systems include a 2,500-amp, 277/480-volt, three-phase main switchboard; four motor control centers for equipment; and several 277/480-volt and 120/208-volt panels for lighting and power. General building lighting is supplied by a combination of incandescent, fluorescent, HID, and exit fixtures.

The facility has a fire alarm annunciator system with smoke detectors and pull stations. A 100 kVA generator with an automatic transfer switch supplies power for the building's emergency systems. The facility also contains intercom, data, cable television, and telephone systems.

Mechanical

The mechanical systems include heating, air conditioning, ventilation, sanitary, domestic water, fire protection, smoke removal, and an elevator. Cooling and heating is supplied by six 25-ton rooftop package units with gas heaters. Air distribution and ventilation are provided via metal-insulated ducts connected to the rooftop package units, air handling units, and fans. An air compressor supplies control air for the pneumatic environmental control system.

The facility has a sanitary and domestic water system. Localized electric hot water heaters supply domestic hot water to the restrooms and lounges. A standpipe and wet pipe sprinkler system meet the building's fire protection requirements. Two roof smoke exhausters provide smoke removal when activated from the fire alarm annunciator system. A hydraulic elevator services the first and second floors.

Equipment and Checklists
Sorted by System

Checklist/System Line No.	Equipment Type	Total Quantity of Each Equipment Type	Annualized Labor-Hours for Each Type of Equipment	Labor-Hours by PM Frequencies for Total Quantities of Equipment — W	M	Q	S	A	Total Annualized Labor-Hours for Each Equipment Type
FIRE PROTECTION									
PM8.2-270-1950	Fire Alarm Annunciator System	1	11.050		4.472	1.118	2.730	2.730	11.050
PM8.2-170-1950	Fire Protection System, Wet Pipe	1	11.341		3.800	2.482	1.241	3.818	11.341
PM8.2-180-1950	Fire Protection Standpipe System	1	4.788		2.976	0.744	0.372	0.696	4.788
PM8.2-295-1950	Fire Protection Valve, OS&Y, 4"+	2	0.423		0.352	0.088	0.044	0.362	0.846
PM8.2-275-1950	Fan, Roof Smoke Exhauster, Up to 42" x 60" & 2 HP	2	2.166		1.456	0.396	1.176	1.176	4.204
CONVEYING									
PM7.1-110-1950	Elevator, Hydraulic, Passenger/Freight	1	10.223		5.040	2.220	1.110	1.853	10.223
COOLING AND HEATING									
PM8.4-850-1950	Package/Rooftop Unit, with Duct Gas Heater	6	4.962			9.468	4.734	15.570	29.772
PM8.4-120-1950	Air Compressor, Reciprocating, Less than 5 HP	1	4.796			2.398	1.199	1.199	4.796
PM8.4-735-1950	Fan, Roof/Wall Exhaust	4	1.176				2.352	2.352	4.704
PLUMBING									
PM8.5-110-1950	Backflow Prevention Device, Up to 4"	1	0.333					0.333	0.333
ELECTRICAL									
PM9.1-150-1950	Switchboard, Electrical	1	0.705					0.705	0.705
PM9.2-110-1950	Motor Control Center, Electric	3	0.389					1.167	1.167
PM9.3-105-2950	Generator, Emergency Diesel, Over 15 kVA	1	16.158		10.216	2.554	1.277	2.111	16.158
PM9.1-210-1950	Automatic Transfer Switch	1	5.316		3.544	0.886	0.443	0.443	5.316

Annualized Labor-Hours by Level

System	Level 1 (Labor-Hours)	Level 2 (Labor-Hours)	Level 3 (Labor-Hours)	Level 4 (Labor-Hours)
FIRE PROTECTION				
Fire Alarm Annunciator System	11.050			
Fire Protection System, Wet Pipe	11.341			
Fire Protection Standpipe System	4.788			
Fire Protection Valve, OS&Y, 4"+	0.846			
Fan, Roof Smoke Exhauster	4.204			
CONVEYING				
Elevator, Hydraulic, Passenger/Freight	10.223			
COOLING AND HEATING				
Package/Rooftop Unit			15.570	14.202
Air Compressor, Reciprocating			2.398	2.398
Fan, Roof/Wall Exhaust			2.352	2.352
PLUMBING				
Backflow Prevention Device			0.333	
ELECTRICAL				
Switchboard, Electrical		0.705		
Motor Control Center, Electric		1.167		
Generator, Emergency Diesel		3.388	2.554	10.216
Automatic Transfer Switch		0.886	0.886	3.544

Annualized (by Level)

	Level 1	Level 2	Level 3	Level 4
	32.229		20.320	18.952
	10.223	6.146	0.333	13.760
			3.440	
	42.452	6.146	24.093	32.712
	8.5	1.2	4.8	6.5

Shop Labor-Hours by Frequency

	W	M	Q	S	A	Total
Fire Protection Shop Labor-Hours by Frequency =		13.056	4.828	5.563	8.782	32.229
Conveying Shop Labor-Hours by Frequency =		5.040	2.220	1.110	1.853	10.223
Heating and Cooling Shop Labor-Hours by Frequency =			11.866	8.285	19.121	39.272
Plumbing Shop Labor-Hours by Frequency =					0.333	0.333
Electric Shop Labor-Hours by Frequency =		13.760	3.440	1.720	4.426	23.346
Total Labor-Hours =		31.856	22.354	16.678	34.515	105.403

Labor-Hours per 10,000 SF = 21.0

Compiled Labor-Hours
- Level 1 = 42.452
- Level 1 - 2 = 48.598
- Level 1 - 3 = 72.691
- Level 1 - 4 = 105.403

Compiled Labor-Hours for 10,000 SF
- Level 1 = 8.5
- Level 1 - 2 = 9.7
- Level 1 - 3 = 14.5
- Level 1 - 4 = 21.0

PERFORMING ARTS CENTER MODEL
1-2 STORIES, 50,000 SF

Part Three

PM STANDARDS/CHECKLISTS

- **Equipment Priority Levels**
- **Maintenance Requirements**
- **Frequencies**

HOW TO USE THE PM STANDARDS/ CHECKLISTS

This section contains the preventive maintenance checklists for individual pieces of equipment or systems commonly found in higher educational facilities. These checklists can be used to establish labor hours and a budget for the PM program. The equipment and systems included in this section correspond with the inventories of the campus building models found in Part Two. The checklists are organized consecutively according to their UniFormat identifying number.

It is necessary to define the PM tasks (checkpoints) and frequencies for each piece of equipment in order to plan, schedule, and ensure that the PM program is accomplished. Again, it is not practical to provide details for every conceivable type of facility and equipment that might be found in an institution of higher education; the systems in this section are representative of most higher education facilities of various sizes.

The PM checklists are based on *Means Facilities Maintenance & Repair Cost Data* (FM&R) and have been customized for the university environment and functional building types. They are intended to provide facility managers with the means to approximate what PM tasks will be done and how often.

Identical pieces of equipment installed in buildings with different operating requirements, or themes, require different PM tasks and different frequencies. The facility manager may also add or tailor any of the PM checklists to fit special operating requirements of a particular facility. Photocopies of individual sheets can be distributed to maintenance personnel to identify the procedures required. The checklists can also be downloaded, customized, and printed from the book's dedicated Website:
http://www.rsmeans.com/supplement/pmhighed.html

The factors that were considered in order to determine which equipment should be included in the PM program, and the frequencies of the PM tasks are: the criticality of the system and/or equipment, the impact of a potential failure on other systems and equipment, and the economic justification for the expense of performing PM. For these reasons, each model has been planned and structured to generally include only those items that meet the objectives delineated above.

Typical PM Checklist

Figure 3.1 is an example of a typical PM Checklist.

1 PM8.4-160-1950
AIR HANDLING UNIT, 3 TO 24 TONS

5

	LABOR-HRS	PM FREQUENCY				
		W	M	Q	S	A
Total labor-hours per event		0.000	0.000	0.420	0.420	0.800
Total labor-hours/year by frequency		0.000	0.000	0.840	0.420	0.800
Total labor-hours/year						2.060
1 Check with operating or area personnel for deficiencies.	0.035			X	X	X
2 Check controls and unit for proper operation.	0.033			X	X	X
3 Check for unusual noise or vibration.	0.033			X	X	X
4 Check tension, condition and alignment of belts; adjust as necessary.	0.029			X	X	X
5 Clean coils, evaporator drain pan, blower, motor and drain piping, as required.	0.380					X
6 Lubricate shaft and motor bearings.	0.047			X	X	X
7 Replace air filters.	0.078			X	X	X
8 Inspect exterior piping and valves for leaks; tighten connections as required.	0.077			X	X	X
9 Clean area around equipment.	0.066			X	X	X
10 Fill out maintenance checklist and report deficiencies.	0.022			X	X	X

FIGURE 3.1

Following is a detailed explanation of the components of the PM checklist:

1 PM Checklist Identification: Each PM checklist is identified by its equipment or system name and a unique identification number based on the UniFormat classification system and Means' own numbering system.

2 PM Tasks: The individual PM operations required to be performed, numbered step by step.

3 Task Labor-Hours: The number of labor-hours required to perform each individual task one time. It should be noted that the hours listed assume that work is being performed by experienced technicians who are familiar with the tasks and are equipped with proper tools and materials.

4 Frequency: Columns are identified with "W" for weekly, "M" for monthly, "Q" for quarterly, "S" for semi-annually, and "A" for annually, which indicate the recommended frequency for performing a task. For example, a check in the "M" column indicates that the task should be performed once each month. In this case, checks will also appear in the "Q," "S," and "A" columns, as these intervals would be covered by a monthly frequency.

5 Total Labor-Hours:

A. Total Labor-Hours per Event: The total labor-hours required to perform all the recommended tasks (indicated with an "X") for a given frequency.

B. Total Labor-Hours/Year by Frequency: The Total Labor-Hours per Event multiplied by the net frequency for each time period.

C. Total Labor-Hours/Year: The annualized labor-hours— the sum of the Total Labor-Hours/Year by Frequency. Annualized labor-hours are based on performing each task at the recommended periodic frequencies in a given year.

Customizing the Checklists

The checklists can be modified to meet the specific needs of your facility. Tasks can be added, modified, deleted, or re-assigned to different frequencies. This will result in changes to the model labor-hour requirements. Figure 3.2 depicts possible modifications to a PM Standard/Checklist to accomodate specific requirements of a particular piece of equipment. A task has been deleted, and Total Labor-Hours per Event, Total Labor-Hours/Year by Frequency, and Total Labor-Hours/Year have all been recalculated.

PM8.4-160-1950
AIR HANDLING UNIT, 3 TO 24 TONS

RESULTING CHANGES

	LABOR-HRS	PM FREQUENCY				
		W	M	Q	S	A
Total labor-hours per event		0.000	0.000	0.343	0.343	0.723
Total labor-hours/year by frequency		0.000	0.000	0.686	0.343	0.723
Total labor-hours/year						1.752
1 Check with operating or area personnel for deficiencies.	0.035			X	X	X
2 Check controls and unit for proper operation.	0.033			X	X	X
3 Check for unusual noise or vibration.	0.033			X	X	X
4 Check tension, condition and alignment of belts; adjust as necessary.	0.029			X	X	X
5 Clean coils, evaporator drain pan, blower, motor and drain piping, as required.	0.380					X
6 Lubricate shaft and motor bearings.	0.047			X	X	X
7 Replace air filters.	0.078			X	X	X
8 Inspect exterior piping and valves for leaks; tighten connections as required.	0.077			X	X	X
9 Clean area around equipment.	0.066			X	X	X
10 Fill out maintenance checklist and report deficiencies.	0.022			X	X	X

DELETED TASK

FIGURE 3.2

66

The following is a list of all PM Standards/Checklists included in this section, organized consecutively according to their UniFormat identifying numbers.

PM7.1-110-1950
ELEVATOR, HYDRAULIC, PASSENGER/FREIGHT

	LABOR-HRS	W	M	Q	S	A
				PM FREQUENCY		
Total labor-hours per event		0.000	0.630	1.110	1.110	1.853
Total labor-hours/year by frequency		0.000	5.040	2.220	1.110	1.853
Total labor-hours/year						10.223
1 Ride car, checking for any unusual noise or operation.	0.052		X	X	X	X
2 In car:						
a) Inspect and clean fixtures and signal in operating panel and car position and direction indicator.	0.103		X	X	X	X
b) Check operation of emergency lights and bell.	0.020		X	X	X	X
c) Check handrails, ceiling panels and hang-on panels for tightness.	0.027		X	X	X	X
d) Check for tripping hazards.	0.012		X	X	X	X
3 Inspect and lubricate rails of hoistway.	0.094		X	X	X	X
4 Hallway corridor:						
a) Inspect hall buttons, signal lamps, lanterns and hall position indicator.	0.046		X	X	X	X
b) Inspect starter station, key operation and lamps.	0.069		X	X	X	X
5 Motor room:						
a) Inspect machine room equipment.	0.077		X	X	X	X
b) Inspect pump and valve unit for leaks.	0.022		X	X	X	X
c) Inspect tank oil level.	0.012		X	X	X	X
d) Inspect and adjust controller contacts, main operating contactors and switches.	0.196			X	X	X
e) Inspect pump and valve unit for leaks.	0.051			X	X	X
f) Inspect and adjust controller overloads; set timers.	0.049					X
g) Tighten connections and clean controller fuses and holders.	0.020					X
h) Inspect and lubricate pump motor bearings.	0.099					X
6 Hatch:						
a) Check hoistway car rails, brackets and fish plates.	0.103					X
b) Inspect/lubricate overhead hatch switches and cams.	0.070					X
c) Inspect/clean/lubricate hatch doors locks, rollers, tracks, upthrusts, relating cables, racks, sight guards and closers, motors, gear boxes, limit and zone switches.	0.096					X
d) Inspect door gibs and fastening.	0.022					X

(Page 1 of 2)

	LABOR-HRS	PM FREQUENCY				
		W	M	Q	S	A
e) Inspect/clean/lubricate cab top guides, steadying devices, safety switches, inductors, leveling devices, selector tape, switches, hitches and fan motor.	0.068					X
f) Check traveling cables for wear.	0.070					X
g) Inspect/clean/lubricate door operator roller tracks, upthrusts, related cables, clutch, retiring cam and door gib.	0.078					X
h) Inspect door operator; clean and lubricate chain and belt tension.	0.052			X	X	X
i) Inspect door; clean and adjust safety edge, light ray and cables.	0.103			X	X	X
j) Clean and adjust proximity devices on door.	0.068			X	X	X
7　Inspect pit gland packing.	0.010			X	X	X
8　Inspect/clean/lubricate under car guides, selector tape, traveling cable, switches and platen plate assembly.	0.068					X
9　Clean equipment and surrounding area.	0.074		X	X	X	X
10　Fill out maintenance checklist and report deficiencies.	0.022		X	X	X	X

(Page 2 of 2)

	LABOR-HRS	PM FREQUENCY				
		W	M	Q	S	A
Total labor-hours per event		0.000	3.061	5.019	5.019	8.068
Total labor-hours/year by frequency		0.000	24.488	10.038	5.019	8.068
Total labor-hours/year						47.613
1 Ride car, checking for any unusual noise or operation.	0.411		X	X	X	X
2 Inspect machine room equipment.	0.286		X	X	X	X
3 Motor room:						
a) Visually inspect controllers and starters.	0.012		X	X	X	X
b) Visually inspect selector.	0.012		X	X	X	X
c) Lubricate and adjust tension of selector.	0.113		X	X	X	X
d) Inspect sleeve bearings of hoist motor.	0.012		X	X	X	X
e) Inspect brushes and commutator of hoist motor.	0.012		X	X	X	X
f) Inspect sleeve bearings of motor generator.	0.012		X	X	X	X
g) Inspect brushes and commutator of motor generator.	0.014		X	X	X	X
h) Inspect sleeve bearings of exciter.			X	X	X	X
i) Inspect brushes and commutator of exciter.	0.022		X	X	X	X
j) Inspect sleeve bearings of regulator dampening motors and tach generators.	0.022		X	X	X	X
k) Inspect brushes and commutator of regulator dampening motors and tach generators.	0.044		X	X	X	X
l) Inspect and grease sleeve bearings of geared machines.	0.047		X	X	X	X
m) Inspect oil level in worm and gear of geared machines.	0.044		X	X	X	X
n) Visually inspect the brakes.	0.022		X	X	X	X
o) Inspect and grease, if necessary, sleeve bearings of drive deflectors and secondary sheaves.	0.186		X	X	X	X
p) Visually inspect and adjust contacts of controllers and starters.	0.338			X	X	X
q) Inspect and adjust main operating contactor and switches of controllers and starters.	0.338			X	X	X
r) Inspect selector, adjusting contacts, brushes and cams if needed.	0.103			X	X	X
s) Inspect selsyn and advancer, motor brushes and commutators of selector.	0.022			X	X	X
t) Clean hoist motor brush rigging and commutator.	0.068			X	X	X
u) Clean motor generator and tighten brush rigging and clean commutator.	0.068			X	X	X
v) Clean exciter brush rigging and commutator.	0.066			X	X	X

(Page 1 of 4)

		PM FREQUENCY				
	LABOR-HRS	W	M	Q	S	A
w) Clean brush rigging and commutator of regulator dampening motors and tach generators.	0.099			X	X	X
x) Inspect machine worm and gear thrust and backlash and spider bolts; replace oil.	0.047			X	X	X
y) Clean and lubricate brakes, pins and linkage.	0.099			X	X	X
z) Inspect governors; lubricate sleeve bearings.	0.099			X	X	X
aa) Inspect controllers and starters; adjust setting of overloads.	0.169					X
ab) Tighten connections on controllers and starters; clean fuses and holders.	0.169					X
ac) Set controllers and starter timers.	0.169					X
ad) Clean controllers and starters.	0.169					X
ae) Clean and inspect selector components.	0.068					X
af) Inspect group operation controllers; clean and lubricate contacts, timers, steppers of operation controller.	0.099					X
ag) Change oil and/or grease roller bearings of the hoist motor.	0.094					X
ah) Vacuum and blowout the hoist motor.	0.094					X
ai) Tighten all connections on the hoist motor.	0.022					X
aj) Change oil and/or grease generator's roller bearings.	0.069					X
ak) Vacuum and blowout motor generator.	0.094					X
al) Inspect all connections on the motor generator and tighten if necessary.	0.022					X
am) Inspect roller bearings of the exciter and change oil and/or grease.	0.069					X
an) Vacuum and blowout exciter.	0.094					X
ao) Change oil and/or grease roller bearings of regulator dampening motors and tach generators.	0.094					X
ap) Vacuum/blowout regulator dampening motors and tach generators.	0.044					X
aq) Inspect all regulator dampening motors and tach generator connections.	0.047					X
ar) Change oil and/or grease roller bearings of the geared machines.	0.094					X
as) Clean and lubricate brake cores.	0.099					X
at) Inspect drive deflectors and secondary sheaves; change oil and grease roller bearings if necessary.	0.170					X
au) Inspect drive deflectors and secondary sheaves' cable grooves for cracks.	0.012					X
av) Inspect governors; change oil and grease roller bearings, if necessary.	0.094					X

(Page 2 of 4)

PM7.1-210-1950
ELEVATOR, CABLE, ELECTRIC, PASSENGER/FREIGHT

	LABOR-HRS	W	M	Q	S	A
4 Hatch:						
a) Lubricate rails of hoistway.	0.733		X	X	X	X
b) Inspect car top and grease sleeve bearings if necessary.	0.151		X	X	X	X
c) Inspect counterweight and grease sleeve bearings if necessary.	0.068		X	X	X	X
d) Visually inspect cables, chains, and hoist compensating governor for wear and equalization.	0.047		X	X	X	X
e) Lubricate cables, chain hoist and compensating governor if necessary.	0.186		X	X	X	X
f) Inspect door operator; clean and lubricate chain and belt tension.	0.177			X	X	X
g) Inspect door; clean and adjust safety edge, light ray and cables.	0.052			X	X	X
h) Clean and adjust proximity devices on door.	0.103			X	X	X
i) Inspect and lubricate governor tape and compensating sheave in pit.	0.068			X	X	X
j) Clean and lubricate compensating tie-down in pit.	0.047			X	X	X
k) Inspect pit's run-by on counterweight.	0.142			X	X	X
l) Inspect governor and compensating sheaves or chains for clearance to pit floor.	0.022			X	X	X
m) Inspect/lubricate overhead hatch switches and cams.	0.096					X
n) Clean and lubricate rollers, cables, sight guards, chains, motors, closures, limit and zone switches.	0.068					X
o) Inspect door gibs and fastening.	0.022					X
5 Inspect car top; change oil and grease roller bearings, if necessary.	0.044					X
6 Check safety switches, indicators, leveling devices, selector tape, switches and hatches.	0.044					X
7 Check and lubricate fan motor.	0.072					X
8 Inspect counterweight; change oil and grease roller bearings, if necessary.	0.094					X
9 Check safety linkage safety and CWT guides.	0.098					X
10 Inspect compensation hatch.	0.047					X
11 Inspect chains, hoists and compensating governor.	0.094					X

(Page 3 of 4)

			PM FREQUENCY				
	LABOR-HRS	W	M	Q	S	A
12 Inspect traveling cables for tracking and wear.	0.070					X
13 Inspect door operator commutator and brushes.	0.012					X
14 Inspect/clean/lubricate door operator clutch, retiring cam, door gib, rollers, tracks, upthrusts and relating cables.	0.103					X
15 Under car:						
a) Inspect/clean/lubricate safety devices, linkages, car guides, selector tape, switches and hitches.	0.020					X
b) Inspect cable hitch and loops; load weighing devices.	0.027					X
16 Inspect/lubricate pit hatch switches, cams and pit oil buffer.	0.083					X
17 In car:						
a) Inspect and clean fixtures and signal in operating panel and car position and direction indicator.	0.103		X	X	X	X
b) Check operation of emergency lights and bells.	0.228		X	X	X	X
c) Check handrails, ceiling panels and hang on panels for tightness.	0.027		X	X	X	X
d) Check for tripping hazards.	0.044		X	X	X	X
18 Hallway corridor:						
a) Inspect hall buttons, signal lamps, lanterns and hall position indicator.	0.046		X	X	X	X
b) Inspect starter station, key operation and lamps.	0.069		X	X	X	X
19 Clean equipment and surrounding area.	0.066		X	X	X	X
20 Fill out maintenance checklist and report deficiencies.	0.022		X	X	X	X

(Page 4 of 4)

PM8.2-170-1950
FIRE PROTECTION SYSTEM, WET PIPE

	LABOR-HRS	PM FREQUENCY				
		W	M	Q	S	A
Total labor-hours per event		0.000	0.475	1.241	1.241	3.818
Total labor-hours/year by frequency		0.000	3.800	2.482	1.241	3.818
Total labor-hours/year						11.341
1 Notify proper authorities prior to testing any alarm systems.	0.130		X	X	X	X
2 Open and close post indicator valve (PIV) to check operation; make minor adjustments such as lubricating valve stem, cleaning and/or replacing target windows as required.	0.176					X
3 Open and close OS&Y (outside stem and yoke) cut-off valve to check operation; make minor repairs such as lubricating stems and tightening packing glands as required.	0.176					X
4 Perform operational test of water flow detectors; make minor adjustments and restore system to proper operating condition.	0.148					X
5 Check to ensure that alarm drain is open; clean drain line if necessary.	0.081		X	X	X	X
6 Open water motor alarm test valve and ensure that outside alarm operates; lubricate alarm, make adjustments as required.	0.176		X	X	X	X
7 Conduct main drain test by opening 2" test valve and observing drop in water pressure on gauge; pressure drop should not exceed 20 psi. Maintain a continuous record of drain tests. Make minor adjustments if applicable. Restore system to proper operating condition.	0.333			X	X	X
8 Check general condition of sprinklers and sprinkler systems; make minor adjustments as required.	0.228					X
9 Check equipment gaskets, piping, packing glands and valves for leaks; tighten flange bolts and loose connections to stop all leaks.	0.013					X

(Page 1 of 2)

	LABOR-HRS	PM FREQUENCY				
		W	M	Q	S	A
10 Check condition of fire department connections; replace missing or broken covers as required.	0.103					X
11 Trip test wet pipe system using test valve furthest from wet pipe valve (control valve). Make minor adjustments as necessary and restore system to proper operating condition.	1.733					X
12 Inspect OS&Y and PIV cut-off valves for open position.	0.066		X	X	X	X
13 Clean area around system components.	0.433			X	X	X
14 Fill out maintenance checklist and report deficiencies.	0.022		X	X	X	X

(Page 2 of 2)

PM8.2-180-1950
FIRE PROTECTION SYSTEM, STANDPIPE

	LABOR-HRS	PM FREQUENCY				
		W	M	Q	S	A
Total labor-hours per event		0.000	0.372	0.372	0.372	0.696
Total labor-hours/year by frequency		0.000	2.976	0.744	0.372	0.696
Total labor-hours/year						4.788
1 Notify proper authorities prior to testing any alarm systems.	0.130		X	X	X	X
2 Open and close OS&Y (outside stem and yoke) cut-off valve to check operation; make minor repairs such as lubricating stems and tightening packing glands as required.	0.176					X
3 Perform operational test of supervisory initiating devices and waterflow detectors; make minor adjustments and restore system to proper operating condition.	0.148					X
4 Check condition of standpipe connections; replace missing and broken covers as required.	0.103		X	X	X	X
5 Ensure that system is set to proper operating condition.	0.051		X	X	X	X
6 Clean area around system components.	0.066		X	X	X	X
7 Fill out maintenance checklist and report deficiencies.	0.022		X	X	X	X

PM8.2-250-1950
FIRE PUMP, ELECTRIC MOTOR DRIVEN

	LABOR-HRS	PM FREQUENCY				
		W	M	Q	S	A
Total labor-hours per event		0.000	1.412	1.412	1.412	1.412
Total labor-hours/year by frequency		0.000	11.296	2.824	1.412	1.412
Total labor-hours/year						16.944
1 Check control panel and wiring for loose connections; tighten connections as required.	0.109		X	X	X	X
2 Ensure all valves relating to water system are in correct position.	0.008		X	X	X	X
3 Open and close OS&Y (outside stem and yoke) cut-off valve to check operation; make minor repairs such as lubricating stems and tightening packing glands as required.	0.176		X	X	X	X
4 Centrifugal pump:						
a) Perform 10 minute pump test run; check for proper operation and adjust if required.	0.217		X	X	X	X
b) Check for leaks on suction and discharge piping, seals, packing glands, etc.	0.077		X	X	X	X
c) Check for excessive vibration, noise, overheating, etc.	0.022		X	X	X	X
d) Check alignment, clearances and rotation of shaft and coupler (includes removing and reinstalling safety cover).	0.160		X	X	X	X
e) Tighten or replace loose, missing or damaged nuts, bolts or screws.	0.005		X	X	X	X
f) Lubricate pump and motor as required.	0.099		X	X	X	X
g) Check suction or discharge pressure gauge readings and flow rate.	0.078		X	X	X	X
h) Check packing glands and tighten or repack as required; note that slight dripping is required for proper lubrication of shaft.	0.113		X	X	X	X
5 Inspect and clean strainers after each use and flow test.	0.260		X	X	X	X
6 Clean equipment and surrounding area.	0.066		X	X	X	X
7 Fill out maintenance checklist and report deficiencies.	0.022		X	X	X	X

PM8.2-270-1950
FIRE ALARM ANNUNCIATOR SYSTEM

	LABOR-HRS	PM FREQUENCY				
		W	M	Q	S	A
Total labor-hours per event		0.000	0.559	0.559	2.730	2.730
Total labor-hours/year by frequency		0.000	4.472	1.118	2.730	2.730
Total labor-hours/year						11.050

#	Task	LABOR-HRS	W	M	Q	S	A
1	Visually inspect all alarm equipment for obstructions or physical damage; clean dirt and dust from interior and exterior of panel/pull boxes and tighten loose connections.	0.222		X	X	X	X
2	Notify proper authorities prior to testing.	0.112		X	X	X	X
3	Conduct operational test of initiating and signal transmitting devices in populated buildings by building zone/area. For those circuits which do not operate properly, check detectors, control units and annunciators for dust on defective components; make minor adjustments as required.	0.112		X	X	X	X
4	Check battery voltages where installed; replace as required.	0.012		X	X	X	X
5	Conduct operational test of 10% of total number of spot-type heat detectors and all smoke detectors. For those circuits which do not operate properly, check to determine if problem relates to circuit, device or control unit; make minor adjustments as required. If detector is defective but no replacement is immediately available, remove detector, re-establish initiating circuit and tag location until a replacement detector is installed.	2.171				X	X
6	Restore system to proper operating condition and notify proper personnel upon completion of tests.	0.079		X	X	X	X
7	Fill out maintenance checklist and report deficiencies.	0.022		X	X	X	X

PM8.2-275-1950
FAN, ROOF SMOKE EXHAUSTER, UP TO 42" X 60" & 2 HP

		LABOR-HRS	PM FREQUENCY				
			W	M	Q	S	A
	Total labor-hours per event		0.000	0.099	0.099	0.588	0.588
	Total labor-hours/year by frequency		0.000	0.792	0.198	0.588	0.588
	Total labor-hours/year						2.166
1	Start and stop fan with local switch.	0.012				X	X
2	Check for loose or missing housing fasteners; tighten or replace as necessary.	0.077		X	X	X	X
3	Check motor and fan shaft bearings for noise, vibration, overheating; lubricate bearings.	0.325				X	X
4	Check belts for wear, tension and alignment, if applicable; adjust as required.	0.057				X	X
5	Check electrical wiring and connections; tighten loose connections.	0.029				X	X
6	Clean fan and surrounding area.	0.066				X	X
7	Fill out maintenance checklist and report deficiencies.	0.022		X	X	X	X

PM8.2-295-1950
VALVE, FIRE PROTECTION, OS&Y, OVER 4"

	LABOR-HRS	PM FREQUENCY				
		W	M	Q	S	A
Total labor-hours per event		0.000	0.022	0.022	0.022	0.181
Total labor-hours/year by frequency		0.000	0.176	0.044	0.022	0.181
Total labor-hours/year						0.423
1 Inspect valve for open position.	0.022		X	X	X	X
2 Lubricate stem; open and close valve to check operation.	0.049					X
3 Check packing gland for leaks; tighten packing and flange bolts as required.	0.022					X
4 Clean valve exterior and surrounding area.	0.066					X
5 Fill out maintenance checklist and report deficiencies.	0.022					X

PM8.3-120-2950
BOILER, HOT WATER; OIL, GAS OR COMBINATION FIRED, 120 TO 500 MBH

	LABOR-HRS	PM FREQUENCY				
		W	M	Q	S	A
Total labor-hours per event		0.000	0.909	1.360	1.360	4.096
Total labor-hours/year by frequency		0.000	7.272	2.720	1.360	4.096
Total labor-hours/year						15.448
1 Check combustion chamber for air or gas leaks.	0.077					X
2 Inspect and clean oil burner gun and ignition assembly where applicable.	0.835					X
3 Inspect fuel system for leaks and change fuel filter element.	0.125					X
4 Check fuel lines and connections for damage.	0.023		X	X	X	X
5 Check for proper operational response of burner to thermostat controls.	0.169			X	X	X
6 Check and lubricate burner and blower motors.	0.099			X	X	X
7 Check main flame failure protection and main flame detection scanner on boiler equipped with spark ignition (oil burner).	0.155		X	X	X	X
8 Check electrical wiring to burner controls and blower.	0.100					X
9 Clean firebox (sweep and vacuum).	0.793					X
10 Check operation of mercury control switches (i.e., steam pressure, hot water temperature limit, atomizing or combustion air proving, etc.).	0.185		X	X	X	X
11 Check operation and condition of safety pressure relief valve.	0.038		X	X	X	X
12 Check operation of boiler low water cut-off devices.	0.070		X	X	X	X
13 Check hot water pressure gauges.	0.073		X	X	X	X

(Page 1 of 2)

PM8.3-120-2950
BOILER, HOT WATER; OIL, GAS OR COMBINATION FIRED, 120 TO 500 MBH

	LABOR-HRS	PM FREQUENCY				
		W	M	Q	S	A
14 Inspect and clean water column sight glass (or replace).	0.160		X	X	X	X
15 Check condition of flue pipe, damper and exhaust stack.	0.183			X	X	X
16 Check boiler operation through complete cycle, up to 30 minutes.	0.806					X
17 Check fuel level with gauge pole; add as required.	0.046		X	X	X	X
18 Clean area around boiler.	0.137		X	X	X	X
19 Fill out maintenance checklist and report deficiencies.	0.022		X	X	X	X

(Page 2 of 2)

PM8.3-120-3950
BOILER, HOT WATER; OIL, GAS OR COMBINATION FIRED, 500 TO 1,000 MBH

	LABOR-HRS	PM FREQUENCY				
		W	M	Q	S	A
Total labor-hours per event		0.000	0.996	1.492	1.492	4.934
Total labor-hours/year by frequency		0.000	7.968	2.984	1.492	4.934
Total labor-hours/year						17.378
1 Check combustion chamber for air or gas leaks.	0.086					X
2 Inspect and clean oil burner gun and ignition assembly where applicable.	0.910					X
3 Inspect fuel system for leaks and change fuel filter element.	0.140					X
4 Check fuel lines and connections for damage.	0.026		X	X	X	X
5 Check for proper operational response of burner to thermostat controls.	0.185			X	X	X
6 Check and lubricate burner and blower motors.	0.109			X	X	X
7 Check main flame failure protection and main flame detection scanner on boiler equipped with spark ignition (oil burner).	0.169		X	X	X	X
8 Check electrical wiring to burner controls and blower.	0.111					X
9 Clean firebox (sweep and vacuum).	0.875					X
10 Check operation of mercury control switches (i.e., steam pressure, hot water temperature limit, atomizing or combustion air proving, etc.).	0.203		X	X	X	X
11 Check operation and condition of safety pressure relief valve.	0.042		X	X	X	X
12 Check operation of boiler low water cut-off devices.	0.077		X	X	X	X
13 Check hot water pressure gauges.	0.081		X	X	X	X
14 Inspect and clean water column sight glass (or replace).	0.176		X	X	X	X

(Page 1 of 2)

		LABOR-HRS	PM FREQUENCY				
			W	M	Q	S	A
15	Clean fire side of water jacket boiler.	0.433					X
16	Check condition of flue pipe, damper and exhaust stack.	0.202			X	X	X
17	Check boiler operation through complete cycle, up to 30 minutes.	0.887					X
18	Check fuel level with gauge pole, add as required.	0.049		X	X	X	X
19	Clean area around boiler.	0.151		X	X	X	X
20	Fill out maintenance checklist and report deficiencies.	0.022		X	X	X	X

(Page 2 of 2)

PM8.3-120-4950
BOILER, HOT WATER; OIL, GAS OR COMBINATION FIRED, OVER 1,000 MBH

		LABOR-HRS	PM FREQUENCY				
			W	M	Q	S	A
	Total labor-hours per event		0.000	1.169	1.709	1.709	5.219
	Total labor-hours/year by frequency		0.000	9.352	3.418	1.709	5.219
	Total labor-hours/year						19.698
1	Check combustion chamber for air or gas leaks.	0.117					X
2	Inspect and clean oil burner gun and ignition assembly where applicable.	0.987					X
3	Inspect fuel system for leaks and change fuel filter element.	0.147					X
4	Check fuel lines and connections for damage.	0.035		X	X	X	X
5	Check for proper operational response of burner to thermostat controls.	0.199			X	X	X
6	Check and lubricate burner and blower motors.	0.120			X	X	X
7	Check main flame failure protection and main flame detection scanner on boiler equipped with spark ignition (oil burner).	0.186		X	X	X	X
8	Check electrical wiring to burner controls and blower.	0.120					X
9	Clean firebox (sweep and vacuum).	0.819					X
10	Check operation of mercury control switches (i.e., steam pressure, hot water temperature limit, atomizing or combustion air proving, etc.).	0.215		X	X	X	X
11	Check operation and condition of safety pressure relief valve.	0.046		X	X	X	X
12	Check operation of boiler low water cut-off devices.	0.085		X	X	X	X
13	Check hot water pressure gauges.	0.109		X	X	X	X
14	Inspect and clean water column sight glass (or replace).	0.191		X	X	X	X
15	Clean fire side of water jacket boiler.	0.433					X

(Page 1 of 2)

PM8.3-120-4950
BOILER, HOT WATER; OIL, GAS OR COMBINATION FIRED, OVER 1,000 MBH

	LABOR-HRS	W	M	Q	S	A
			PM FREQUENCY			
16 Check condition of flue pipe, damper and exhaust stack.	0.221			X	X	X
17 Check boiler operation through complete cycle, up to 30 minutes.	0.887					X
18 Check fuel level with gauge pole, add as required.	0.098		X	X	X	X
19 Clean area around boiler.	0.182		X	X	X	X
20 Fill out maintenance checklist and report deficiencies.	0.022		X	X	X	X

(Page 2 of 2)

PM8.3-160-4950
BOILER, STEAM; OIL, GAS OR COMBINATION FIRED, OVER 1,000 MBH

	LABOR-HRS	PM FREQUENCY				
		W	M	Q	S	A
Total labor-hours per event		0.000	1.038	2.645	2.645	6.211
Total labor-hours/year by frequency		0.000	8.304	5.290	2.645	6.211
Total labor-hours/year						22.450
1 Inspect fuel system for leaks or damage.	0.098		X	X	X	X
2 Change fuel filter element and strainers; repair leaks.	1.027					X
3 Check main flame failure protection, positive fuel shutoff and main flame detection scanner on boiler equipped with spark ignition (oil burner).	0.147		X	X	X	X
4 Check for proper operational response of burner to thermostat controls.	0.199			X	X	X
5 Inspect all gas, steam and water lines, valves, connections for leaks or damage; repair as necessary.	0.195			X	X	X
6 Check feedwater system and feedwater makeup control and pump.	0.091		X	X	X	X
7 Check and lubricate burner, blowers and motors as required.	0.120			X	X	X
8 Check operation and condition of safety pressure relief valve.	0.069		X	X	X	X
9 Check combustion controls, combustion blower and damper modulation control.	0.199					X
10 Check all indicator lamps and water/steam pressure gauges.	0.109		X	X	X	X
11 Check electrical panels and wiring to burner, blowers and other components.	0.140			X	X	X
12 Clean or replace air-intake louvers, if required.	0.069			X	X	X
13 Check condition of flue pipe, damper and exhaust stack.	0.147		X	X	X	X
14 Check boiler operation through complete cycle, up to 30 minutes.	0.884			X	X	X

(Page 1 of 2)

PM8.3-160-4950
BOILER, STEAM; OIL, GAS OR COMBINATION FIRED, OVER 1,000 MBH

		LABOR-HRS	PM FREQUENCY				
			W	M	Q	S	A
15	Check water column sight glass and water level system; clean or replace sight glass, if required.	0.127		X	X	X	X
16	Clean firebox (sweep and vacuum).	1.144					X
17	Check fuel level with gauge pole for oil burning boilers.	0.046		X	X	X	X
18	Inspect and clean oil burner gun and ignition assembly where applicable.	1.196					X
19	Clean area around boiler.	0.182		X	X	X	X
20	Fill out maintenance checklist and report deficiencies.	0.022		X	X	X	X

(Page 2 of 2)

PM8.3-160-4975
BOILER, STEAM; OIL, GAS OR COMBINATION FIRED, OVER 1,000 MBH, SPECIAL

(Supplies heat for building and pool water.)

	LABOR-HRS	PM FREQUENCY				
		W	M	Q	S	A
Total labor-hours per event		0.295	1.237	2.645	2.645	6.211
Total labor-hours/year by frequency		11.800	9.896	5.290	2.645	6.211
Total labor-hours/year						35.842
1 Inspect fuel system for leaks or damage.	0.098		X	X	X	X
2 Change fuel filter element and strainers; repair leaks.	1.027					X
3 Check main flame mailure protections, positive fuel shutoff and main flame detection scanner on boiler equipped with spark ignition (oil burner).	0.147		X	X	X	X
4 Check for proper operational response of burner to thermostat controls.	0.199		X	X	X	X
5 Inspect all gas, steam and water lines; valves; and connections for leaks or damage. Repair as necessary.	0.195			X	X	X
6 Check feedwater system and feedwater makeup control and pump.	0.091	X	X	X	X	X
7 Check and lubricate burner, blowers and motors as required.	0.120			X	X	X
8 Check operation and condition of safety pressure relief valve.	0.069		X	X	X	X
9 Check combustion controls, combustion blower and damper modulation control.	0.199					X
10 Check all indicator lamps and water/steam pressure gauges.	0.109		X	X	X	X
11 Check electrical panels and wiring to burner, blowers and other components.	0.140			X	X	X
12 Clean or replace air-intake louvers, if required.	0.069			X	X	X
13 Check condition of flue pipe, damper and exhaust stack.	0.147		X	X	X	X
14 Check boiler operation through complete cycle, up to 30 minutes.	0.884			X	X	X

(Page 1 of 2)

	LABOR-HRS	PM FREQUENCY				
		W	M	Q	S	A
15 Check water column sight glass and water level system; clean or replace sight glass, if required.	0.127		X	X	X	X
16 Clean firebox (sweep and vacuum).	1.144					X
17 Check fuel level with gauge pole for oil-burning boilers.	0.046		X	X	X	X
18 Inspect and clean oil burner gun and ignition assembly where applicable.	1.196					X
19 Clean area around boiler.	0.182	X	X	X	X	X
20 Fill out maintenance checklist and report deficiencies.	0.022	X	X	X	X	X

(Page 2 of 2)

PM8.3-710-3950
PUMP, STEAM CONDENSATE RETURN, DUPLEX

	LABOR-HRS	PM FREQUENCY				
		W	M	Q	S	A
Total labor-hours per event		0.000	0.000	0.000	0.571	0.571
Total labor-hours/year by frequency		0.000	0.000	0.000	0.571	0.571
Total labor-hours/year						1.142
1 Check with operating or area personnel for deficiencies.	0.035				X	X
2 Check for proper operation.	0.022				X	X
3 Check for leaks on suction and discharge piping, seals, packing glands, etc.; make minor adjustments as required.	0.153				X	X
4 Check pumps and motors operation for excessive vibration, noise and overheating.	0.044				X	X
5 Check pump controller for proper operation.	0.130				X	X
6 Lubricate pumps and motors.	0.099				X	X
7 Clean condensate return unit and surrounding area.	0.066				X	X
8 Fill out maintenance checklist and report deficiencies.	0.022				X	X

PM8.4-015-1950
CENTRIFUGAL PUMP, OVER 1 HP

	LABOR-HRS	PM FREQUENCY				
		W	M	Q	S	A
Total labor-hours per event		0.000	0.000	0.000	0.598	0.598
Total labor-hours/year by frequency		0.000	0.000	0.000	0.598	0.598
Total labor-hours/year						1.196
1 Check for proper operation of pump.	0.022				X	X
2 Check for leaks on suction and discharge piping, seals, packing glands, etc.; make minor adjustments as required.	0.077				X	X
3 Check pump and motor operation for excessive vibration, noise and overheating.	0.022				X	X
4 Check alignment of pump and motor; adjust as necessary.	0.260				X	X
5 Lubricate pump and motor.	0.099				X	X
6 Clean exterior of pump, motor and surrounding area.	0.096				X ·	X
7 Fill out maintenance checklist and report deficiencies.	0.022				X	X

PM8.4-020-1950
PUMP, STORM WATER, SIMPLEX LIFT STATION

	LABOR-HRS	PM FREQUENCY				
		W	M	Q	S	A
Total labor-hours per event		0.000	0.000	0.000	0.000	2.537
Total labor-hours/year by frequency		0.000	0.000	0.000	0.000	2.537
Total labor-hours/year						2.537
1 Check with operating or area personnel for deficiencies.	0.035					X
2 Remove pump from pit.	0.585					X
3 Check for trash in pit; remove if required.	0.062					X
4 Clean out trash from pump intake.	0.338					X
5 Inspect pump body for corrosion; prime and paint as necessary.	0.053					X
6 Check pump and motor operation for excessive vibration, noise and overheating.	0.044					X
7 Check coupling and alignment of pump and motor; adjust as necessary.	0.520					X
8 Lubricate pump and motor.	0.098					X
9 Return pump to pit; reset and check float switches and alarm for proper operation.	0.585					X
10 Check float switches for operation and sequencing.	0.022					X
11 Reinstall loose or removed access panels.	0.077					X
12 Clean exterior of lift station and surrounding area.	0.096					X
13 Fill out maintenance checklist and report deficiencies.	0.022					X

PM8.4-020-2950
PUMP, STORM WATER, DUPLEX LIFT STATION

	LABOR-HRS	PM FREQUENCY				
		W	M	Q	S	A
Total labor-hours per event		0.000	0.000	0.000	0.000	4.196
Total labor-hours/year by frequency		0.000	0.000	0.000	0.000	4.196
Total labor-hours/year						4.196
1 Check with operating or area personnel for deficiencies.	0.035					X
2 Remove pumps from pit.	1.170					X
3 Check for trash in pit; remove if required.	0.062					X
4 Clean out trash from pump intake.	0.676					X
5 Inspect pump bodies for corrosion; prime and paint as necessary.	0.106					X
6 Check pumps and motors operation for excessive vibration, noise and overheating.	0.044					X
7 Check coupling and alignment of pump and motor; adjust as necessary.	0.520					X
8 Lubricate pumps and motors.	0.196					X
9 Return pumps to pit; reset and check float switches and alarm for proper operation.	1.170					X
10 Check float switches for operation and sequencing.	0.022					X
11 Reinstall loose or removed access panels.	0.077					X
12 Clean exterior of pumps, motors and surrounding area.	0.096					X
13 Fill out maintenance checklist and report deficiencies.	0.022					X

PM8.4-120-1950
AIR COMPRESSOR, RECIPROCATING,
LESS THAN 5 HP

	LABOR-HRS	PM FREQUENCY				
		W	M	Q	S	A
Total labor-hours per event		0.000	0.000	1.199	1.199	1.199
Total labor-hours/year by frequency		0.000	0.000	2.398	1.199	1.199
Total labor-hours/year						4.796
1 Replace compressor oil.	0.341			X	X	X
2 Perform operation check of compressor system and adjust as required.	0.221			X	X	X
3 Check motor operation for excessive vibration, noise and overheating.	0.042			X	X	X
4 Lubricate motor.	0.047			X	X	X
5 Check operation of pressure relief valve.	0.030			X	X	X
6 Check tension, condition and alignment of v-belts; adjust as necessary.	0.030			X	X	X
7 Drain moisture from air storage tank and check low pressure cut-in. While draining, check discharge for indication of interior corrosion.	0.046			X	X	X
8 Clean air-intake filter on compressor.	0.177			X	X	X
9 Clean oil and water trap.	0.177			X	X	X
10 Clean exterior of compressor, motor and surrounding area.	0.066			X	X	X
11 Fill out maintenance checklist and report deficiencies.	0.022			X	X	X

PM8.4-120-2950
AIR COMPRESSOR, RECIPROCATING, 5 TO 40 HP

	LABOR-HRS	PM FREQUENCY				
		W	M	Q	S	A
Total labor-hours per event		0.000	0.000	1.214	1.214	1.214
Total labor-hours/year by frequency		0.000	0.000	2.428	1.214	1.214
Total labor-hours/year						4.856
1 Replace compressor oil.	0.341			X	X	X
2 Perform operation check of compressor system and adjust as required.	0.221			X	X	X
3 Check motor operation for excessive vibration, noise and overheating; lubricate motor.	0.042			X	X	X
4 Check operation of pressure relief valve.	0.043			X	X	X
5 Clean cooling fans and air cooler on compressor.	0.023			X	X	X
6 Check tension, condition and alignment of v-belts; adjust as necessary.	0.030			X	X	X
7 Drain moisture from air storage tank and check low pressure cut-in. While draining, check discharge for indication of interior corrosion.	0.059			X	X	X
8 Clean air-intake filter on compressor.	0.177			X	X	X
9 Clean oil and water trap.	0.190			X	X	X
10 Clean compressor and surrounding area.	0.066			X	X	X
11 Fill out maintenance checklist and report deficiencies.	0.022			X	X	X

PM8.4-160-1950
AIR HANDLING UNIT, 3 TO 24 TONS

		LABOR-HRS	PM FREQUENCY				
			W	M	Q	S	A
Total labor-hours per event			0.000	0.000	0.420	0.420	0.800
Total labor-hours/year by frequency			0.000	0.000	0.840	0.420	0.800
Total labor-hours/year							2.060
1	Check with operating or area personnel for deficiencies.	0.035			X	X	X
2	Check controls and unit for proper operation.	0.033			X	X	X
3	Check for unusual noise or vibration.	0.033			X	X	X
4	Check tension, condition and alignment of belts; adjust as necessary.	0.029			X	X	X
5	Clean coils, evaporator drain pan, blower, motor and drain piping, as required.	0.380					X
6	Lubricate shaft and motor bearings.	0.047			X	X	X
7	Replace air filters.	0.078			X	X	X
8	Inspect exterior piping and valves for leaks; tighten connections as required.	0.077			X	X	X
9	Clean area around equipment.	0.066			X	X	X
10	Fill out maintenance checklist and report deficiencies.	0.022			X	X	X

AIR HANDLING UNIT, 3 TO 24 TONS, SPECIAL

	LABOR-HRS	PM FREQUENCY				
		W	M	Q	S	A
Total labor-hours per event		0.000	0.201	0.420	0.420	0.800
Total labor-hours/year by frequency		0.000	1.608	0.840	0.420	0.800
Total labor-hours/year						3.668
1 Check with operating or area personnel for deficiencies.	0.035		X	X	X	X
2 Check controls and unit for proper operation.	0.033		X	X	X	X
3 Check for unusual noise or vibration.	0.033		X	X	X	X
4 Check tension, condition and alignment of belts; adjust as necessary.	0.029			X	X	X
5 Clean coils, evaporator drain pan, blower, motor and drain piping, as required.	0.380					X
6 Lubricate shaft and motor bearings.	0.047			X	X	X
7 Replace air filters.	0.078		X	X	X	X
8 Inspect exterior piping and valves for leaks; tighten connections as required.	0.077			X	X	X
9 Clean area around equipment.	0.066			X	X	X
10 Fill out maintenance checklist and report deficiencies.	0.022		X	X	X	X

PM8.4-160-2950
AIR HANDLING UNIT, 25 TO 50 TONS

	LABOR-HRS	PM FREQUENCY				
		W	M	Q	S	A
Total labor-hours per event		0.000	0.000	0.420	0.420	0.878
Total labor-hours/year by frequency		0.000	0.000	0.840	0.420	0.878
Total labor-hours/year						2.138
1 Check with operating or area personnel for deficiencies.	0.035			X	X	X
2 Check controls and unit for proper operation.	0.033			X	X	X
3 Check for unusual noise or vibration.	0.033			X	X	X
4 Clean coils, evaporator drain pan, blower, motor and drain piping, as required.	0.380					X
5 Lubricate shaft and motor bearings.	0.047			X	X	X
6 Check belts for wear, proper tension and alignment; adjust as necessary.	0.029			X	X	X
7 Inspect exterior piping and valves for leaks; tighten connections as required.	0.077			X	X	X
8 Check operation and clean dampers, louvers and shutters; lubricate all pivot points and linkages.	0.078					X
9 Replace air filters.	0.078			X	X	X
10 Clean area around equipment.	0.066			X	X	X
11 Fill out maintenance checklist and report deficiencies.	0.022			X	X	X

PM8.4-160-2975
AIR HANDLING UNIT, 25 TO 50 TONS, SPECIAL

	LABOR-HRS	PM FREQUENCY				
		W	M	Q	S	A
Total labor-hours per event		0.000	0.201	0.420	0.420	0.878
Total labor-hours/year by frequency		0.000	1.608	0.840	0.420	0.878
Total labor-hours/year						3.746
1 Check with operating or area personnel for deficiencies.	0.035		X	X	X	X
2 Check controls and unit for proper operation.	0.033		X	X	X	X
3 Check for unusual noise or vibration.	0.033		X	X	X	X
4 Clean coils, evaporator drain pan, blower, motor and drain piping, as required.	0.380					X
5 Lubricate shaft and motor bearings.	0.047			X	X	X
6 Check belts for wear, proper tension, and alignment; adjust as necessary.	0.029			X	X	X
7 Inspect exterior piping and valves for leaks; tighten connections as required.	0.077			X	X	X
8 Check operation and clean dampers, louvers and shutters; lubricate pivot points and linkages.	0.078					X
9 Replace air filters.	0.078		X	X	X	X
10 Clean area around equipment.	0.066			X	X	X
11 Fill out maintenance checklist and report deficiencies.	0.022		X	X	X	X

PM8.4-220-2950
CHILLER, CENTRIFUGAL, WATER COOLED, OVER 100 TONS

	LABOR-HRS	PM FREQUENCY				
		W	M	Q	S	A
Total labor-hours per event		0.280	1.155	1.155	1.288	9.886
Total labor-hours/year by frequency		11.200	9.240	2.310	1.288	9.886
Total labor-hours/year						33.924
1 Check unit for proper operation.	0.035	X	X	X	X	X
2 Check oil level; add oil as necessary.	0.022	X	X	X	X	X
3 Check oil temperature.	0.038	X	X	X	X	X
4 Check dehydrator or purge system; remove water if observed in sight glass.	0.046	X	X	X	X	X
5 Run system control tests.	0.455		X	X	X	X
6 Check refrigerant charge/level; add as necessary.	0.381		X	X	X	X
7 Check compressor for excessive noise/vibration.	0.039		X	X	X	X
8 Check sensor and mechanical safety limits; replace as necessary.	0.133				X	X
9 Clean dehydrator float valve.	0.351					X
10 Perform spectrochemical analysis of compressor oil; replace oil as necessary.	0.039					X
11 Replace oil filters and add oil as necessary.	0.161					X
12 Inspect cooler and condenser tubes for leaks; clean screens as necessary.	5.200					X
13 Inspect utility vessel vent piping and safety relief valve; replace as necessary.	0.247					X
14 Inspect/clean the economizer (vane) gas line, damper valve and actuator arm.	0.650					X
15 Run an insulation test on the centrifugal motor.	1.950					X
16 Clean area around equipment.	0.117	X	X	X	X	X
17 Document all maintenance and cleaning procedures.	0.022	X	X	X	X	X

PM8.4-230-2950
CHILLER, RECIPROCATING, AIR COOLED, OVER 25 TONS

	LABOR-HRS	PM FREQUENCY				
		W	M	Q	S	A
Total labor-hours per event		0.000	0.874	0.874	0.874	3.273
Total labor-hours/year by frequency		0.000	6.992	1.748	0.874	3.273
Total labor-hours/year						12.887
1 Check unit for proper operation, excessive noise or vibration.	0.033		X	X	X	X
2 Run system diagnostics test.	0.455		X	X	X	X
3 Check oil level in sight glass of lead compressor only; add oil as necessary.	0.042		X	X	X	X
4 Check superheat and subcooling temperatures.	0.325					X
5 Check liquid line sight glass, oil and refrigerant pressures.	0.036		X	X	X	X
6 Check contactors, sensors and mechanical safety limits.	0.094					X
7 Check electrical wiring and connections; tighten loose connections.	0.120					X
8 Clean intake side of condenser coils, fans and intake screens.	1.282					X
9 Inspect fan(s) or blower(s) for bent blades or imbalance.	0.237					X
10 Lubricate shaft bearings and motor bearings as required.	0.341					X
11 Inspect plumbing and valves for leaks, adjust as necessary.	0.117		X	X	X	X
12 Check evaporator and condenser for corrosion.	0.052		X	X	X	X
13 Clean chiller and surrounding area.	0.117		X	X	X	X
14 Fill out maintenance checklist and report deficiencies.	0.022		X	X	X	X

105

PM8.4-240-2950
CHILLER, RECIPROCATING, WATER COOLED, OVER 50 TONS

	LABOR-HRS	PM FREQUENCY				
		W	M	Q	S	A
Total labor-hours per event		0.000	0.874	0.874	0.874	1.293
Total labor-hours/year by frequency		0.000	6.992	1.748	0.874	1.293
Total labor-hours/year						10.907
1 Check unit for proper operation, excessive noise or vibration.	0.033		X	X	X	X
2 Run system diagnostics test.	0.455		X	X	X	X
3 Check oil level in sight glass of lead compressor only; add oil as necessary.	0.042		X	X	X	X
4 Check superheat and subcooling temperatures.	0.325					X
5 Check liquid line sight glass, oil and refrigerant pressures.	0.036		X	X	X	X
6 Check contactors, sensors and mechanical limits; adjust as necessary.	0.094					X
7 Inspect plumbing and valves for leaks; tighten connections as necessary.	0.117		X	X	X	X
8 Check condenser and evaporator for corrosion.	0.052		X	X	X	X
9 Clean chiller and surrounding area.	0.117		X	X	X	X
10 Fill out maintenance checklist and report deficiencies.	0.022		X	X	X	X

PM8.4-510-2950
COOLING TOWER, FORCED DRAFT, 50 TO 499 TONS

	LABOR-HRS	PM FREQUENCY				
		W	M	Q	S	A
Total labor-hours per event		0.000	0.000	0.000	4.956	4.956
Total labor-hours/year by frequency		0.000	0.000	0.000	4.956	4.956
Total labor-hours/year						9.912
1 Check with operating or area personnel for deficiencies.	0.074				X	X
2 Check operation of unit for water leaks, noise or vibration.	0.163				X	X
3 Clean and inspect hot water basin.	0.332				X	X
4 Remove access panel.	0.103				X	X
5 Check electrical wiring and connections; make appropriate adjustments.	0.255				X	X
6 Lubricate all motor and fan bearings.	0.100				X	X
7 Check fan blades or blowers for imbalance and tip clearance.	0.247				X	X
8 Check belt for wear, tension and alignment; adjust as required.	0.096				X	X
9 Drain and flush cold water sump and clean strainer.	0.819				X	X
10 Clean inside of water tower using water hose; scrape, brush and wipe as required. Heavy deposits of scale should be removed with scale-removing compound.	1.271				X	X
11 Refill with water; check make-up water assembly for leakage. Adjust float if necessary.	0.447				X	X
12 Replace access panel.	0.078				X	X
13 Remove, clean and reinstall conductivity and pH electrodes in chemical water treatment system.	0.832				X	X
14 Inspect and clean around cooling tower.	0.117				X	X
15 Fill out maintenance checklist and report deficiencies.	0.022				X	X

PM8.4-510-3950
COOLING TOWER, FORCED DRAFT, 500 TO 1,000 TONS

	LABOR-HRS	PM FREQUENCY				
		W	M	Q	S	A
Total labor-hours per event		0.000	0.000	0.000	8.864	8.864
Total labor-hours/year by frequency		0.000	0.000	0.000	8.864	8.864
Total labor-hours/year						17.728
1 Check with operating or area personnel for deficiencies.	0.109				X	X
2 Check operation of unit for water leaks, noise or vibration.	0.239				X	X
3 Clean and inspect hot water basin.	0.488				X	X
4 Remove access panel.	0.151				X	X
5 Check electrical wiring and connections; make appropriate adjustments.	0.374				X	X
6 Lubricate all motor and fan bearings.	0.147				X	X
7 Check fan blades or blowers for imbalance and tip clearance.	0.302				X	X
8 Check belt for wear, tension and alignment; adjust as required.	0.22				X	X
9 Drain and flush cold water sump and clean strainer.	1.464				X	X
10 Clean inside of water tower using water hose; scrape, brush and wipe as required. Heavy deposits of scale should be removed with scale-removing compound.	2.259				X	X
11 Refill with water; check make-up water assembly for leakage. Adjust float if necessary.	1.578				X	X
12 Replace access panel.	0.117				X	X
13 Remove, clean and reinstall conductivity and pH electrodes in chemical water treatment system.	1.222				X	X
14 Inspect and clean around cooling tower.	0.172				X	X
15 Fill out maintenance checklist and report deficiencies.	0.022				X	X

PM8.4-710-3950
FAN, AXIAL, 36" TO 48" DIAMETER
(OVER 10,000 CFM)

	LABOR-HRS	PM FREQUENCY				
		W	M	Q	S	A
Total labor-hours per event		0.000	0.000	0.000	0.695	0.695
Total labor-hours/year by frequency		0.000	0.000	0.000	0.695	0.695
Total labor-hours/year						1.390
1 Start and stop fan with local switch.	0.012				X	X
2 Check motor and fan shaft bearings for noise, vibration, overheating; lubricate bearings.	0.325				X	X
3 Check belts for wear, tension and alignment, if applicable; adjust as required.	0.086				X	X
4 Check fan pitch operator; lubricate, if applicable.	0.029				X	X
5 Check electrical wiring and connections; tighten loose connections.	0.078				X	X
6 Clean fan and surrounding area.	0.143				X	X
7 Fill out maintenance checklist and report deficiencies.	0.022				X	X

109

PM8.4-710-3975
FAN, AXIAL, 36" TO 48" DIAMETER
(OVER 10,000 CFM), SPECIAL

	LABOR-HRS	PM FREQUENCY				
		W	M	Q	S	A
Total labor-hours per event		0.000	0.000	0.050	0.711	0.711
Total labor-hours/year by frequency		0.000	0.000	0.100	0.711	0.711
Total labor-hours/year						1.522
1 Start and stop fan with local switch.	0.012			X	X	X
2 Check motor and fan shaft bearings for noise, vibration, overheating; lubricate bearings.	0.325				X	X
3 Check unit for proper operation, noise, and vibration.	0.016			X	X	X
4 Check belts for wear, tension, and alignment, if applicable; adjust as required.	0.086				X	X
5 Check fan pitch operator; lubricate, if applicable.	0.029				X	X
6 Check electrical wiring and connections; tighten loose connections.	0.078				X	X
7 Clean fan and surrounding area.	0.143				X	X
8 Fill out maintenance checklist and report deficiencies.	0.022			X	X	X

110

PM8.4-735-1950
FAN, ROOF/WALL EXHAUST

	LABOR-HRS	PM FREQUENCY				
		W	M	Q	S	A
Total labor-hours per event		0.000	0.000	0.000	0.588	0.588
Total labor-hours/year by frequency		0.000	0.000	0.000	0.588	0.588
Total labor-hours/year						1.176
1 Start and stop fan with local switch.	0.012				X	X
2 Check for loose or missing housing fasteners; tighten or replace as necessary.	0.077				X	X
3 Check motor and fan shaft bearings for noise, vibration, overheating; lubricate bearings.	0.325				X	X
4 Check belts for wear, tension and alignment, if applicable; adjust as required.	0.057				X	X
5 Check electrical wiring and connections; tighten loose connections.	0.029				X	X
6 Clean fan and surrounding area.	0.066				X	X
7 Fill out maintenance checklist and report deficiencies.	0.022				X	X

111

PM8.4-740-1950
FAN, FUME HOOD, UTILITY, EXHAUST

	LABOR-HRS	PM FREQUENCY				
		W	M	Q	S	A
Total labor-hours per event		0.000	0.376	0.376	0.540	0.540
Total labor-hours/year by frequency		0.000	3.008	0.752	0.540	0.540
Total labor-hours/year						4.840
1 Start and stop fan with local switch.	0.012				X	X
2 Check motor and fan shaft bearings for noise, vibration, overheating; lubricate bearings.	0.325		X	X	X	X
3 Check belts for wear, tension and alignment, if applicable; adjust as required.	0.057				X	X
4 Check flexible duct connectors.	0.029		X	X	X	X
5 Check electrical wiring and connections; tighten loose connections.	0.029				X	X
6 Clean fan and surrounding area.	0.066				X	X
7 Fill out maintenance checklist and report deficiencies.	0.022		X	X	X	X

PM8.4-760-1950
FLUID COOLER, 2 FANS (NO COMPRESSOR)

	LABOR-HRS	PM FREQUENCY				
		W	M	Q	S	A
Total labor-hours per event		0.000	0.000	0.000	0.000	1.123
Total labor-hours/year by frequency		0.000	0.000	0.000	0.000	1.123
Total labor-hours/year						1.123
1 Check with operating or area personnel for deficiencies.	0.035					X
2 Check unit for proper operation, excessive noise or vibration.	0.159					X
3 Clean intake side of condenser coils, fans and intake screens.	0.473					X
4 Check electrical wiring and connections; tighten loose connections.	0.120					X
5 Inspect fan(s) for bent blades or unbalance; adjust as necessary.	0.040					X
6 Check belts for condition, proper tension and misalignment; adjust for proper tension and/or alignment, if required.	0.029					X
7 Lubricate shaft bearings and motor bearings.	0.047					X
8 Inspect piping and valves for leaks; tighten connections as necessary.	0.077					X
9 Lubricate and check operation of dampers, if applicable.	0.055					X
10 Clean area around fluid cooler.	0.066					X
11 Fill out maintenance checklist and report deficiencies.	0.022					X

PM8.4-810-1950
PACKAGE/ROOFTOP UNIT, AIR COOLED, 3 TO 24 TONS

		LABOR-HRS	PM FREQUENCY				
			W	M	Q	S	A
	Total labor-hours per event		0.000	0.000	0.466	0.466	1.004
	Total labor-hours/year by frequency		0.000	0.000	0.932	0.466	1.004
	Total labor-hours/year						2.402
1	Check with operating or area personnel for deficiencies.	0.035			X	X	X
2	Check tension, condition and alignment of belts; adjust as necessary.	0.029			X	X	X
3	Lubricate shaft and motor bearings.	0.047			X	X	X
4	Replace air filters.	0.055			X	X	X
5	Clean electrical wiring and connections; tighten loose connections.	0.120					X
6	Clean coils, evaporator drain pan, blowers, fans, motors and drain piping as required.	0.385					X
7	Perform operational check of unit; make adjustments on controls and other components as required.	0.077			X	X	X
8	During operation of unit, check refrigerant pressure; add refrigerant as necessary.	0.135			X	X	X
9	Check compressor oil level; add oil as required.	0.033					X
10	Clean area around unit.	0.066			X	X	X
11	Fill out maintenance checklist and report deficiencies.	0.022			X	X	X

PM8.4-840-1950
PACKAGE UNIT, COMPUTER ROOM

	LABOR-HRS	PM FREQUENCY				
		W	M	Q	S	A
Total labor-hours per event		0.000	0.000	0.759	1.409	1.409
Total labor-hours/year by frequency		0.000	0.000	1.518	1.409	1.409
Total labor-hours/year						4.336
1 Check with operating or area personnel for deficiencies.	0.035			X	X	X
2 Run microprocessor check, if available, or check controls and unit for proper operation.	0.216			X	X	X
3 Check for unusual noise or vibration.	0.033			X	X	X
4 Clean coils, evaporator drain pan, humidifier pan, blower, motor and drain piping as required.	0.380				X	X
5 Replace air filters.	0.078			X	X	X
6 Lubricate shaft and motor bearings.	0.047			X	X	X
7 Check belts for wear, proper tension and alignment; adjust as necessary.	0.029			X	X	X
8 Check humidity lamp; replace if necessary.	0.156			X	X	X
9 During operation of unit, check refrigerant pressures; add refrigerant as necessary.	0.270				X	X
10 Inspect exterior piping and valves for leaks; tighten connections as required.	0.077			X	X	X
11 Clean area around unit.	0.066			X	X	X
12 Fill out maintenance checklist and report deficiencies.	0.022			X	X	X

PM8.4-850-1950
PACKAGE/ROOFTOP UNIT WITH DUCT GAS HEATER

	LABOR-HRS	PM FREQUENCY				
		W	M	Q	S	A
Total labor-hours per event		0.000	0.000	0.789	0.789	2.595
Total labor-hours/year by frequency		0.000	0.000	1.578	0.789	2.595
Total labor-hours/year						4.962
1 Check with operating or area personnel for deficiencies.	0.035			X	X	X
2 Check tension, condition and alignment of belts; adjust as necessary.	0.029			X	X	X
3 Lubricate shaft and motor bearings.	0.047			X	X	X
4 Replace air filters.	0.078			X	X	X
5 Check electrical wiring and connections; tighten loose connections.	0.120					X
6 Clean coils, evaporator drain pan, blowers, fans, motors and drain piping as required.	0.385					X
7 Perform operational check of unit; make adjustments on controls and other components as required.	0.077			X	X	X
8 During operation of unit, check refrigerant pressures; add refrigerant as necessary.	0.272			X	X	X
9 Check compressor oil level; add oil as required.	0.033					X
10 Inspect, clean and adjust control valves and thermo-sensing bulbs on gas burners.	0.254					X

(Page 1 of 2)

116

PM8.4-850-1950
PACKAGE/ROOFTOP UNIT WITH
DUCT GAS HEATER

	LABOR-HRS	PM FREQUENCY				
		W	M	Q	S	A
11 Inspect fuel system for leaks.	0.016			X	X	X
12 Check for proper operation of burner primary controls. Check and adjust thermostat.	0.133					X
13 Check electrical wiring to burner controls.	0.079					X
14 Inspect and clean firebox.	0.577					X
15 Check condition of flue pipe, damper and stack.	0.147			X	X	X
16 Check heater operation through complete cycle or up to 10 minutes.	0.225					X
17 Clean area around entire unit.	0.066			X	X	X
18 Fill out maintenance checklist and report deficiencies.	0.022			X	X	X

(Page 2 of 2)

PM8.5-110-1950
BACKFLOW PREVENTION DEVICE, UP TO 4"
(Note: Test frequency may vary depending on local regulations and application.)

	LABOR-HRS	PM FREQUENCY				
		W	M	Q	S	A
Total labor-hours per event		0.000	0.000	0.000	0.000	0.333
Total labor-hours/year by frequency		0.000	0.000	0.000	0.000	0.333
Total labor-hours/year						0.333
1 Test and calibrate check valve operation with test set.	0.191					X
2 Bleed air from backflow preventer.	0.047					X
3 Inspect for leaks under pressure.	0.007					X
4 Clean backflow preventer and surrounding area.	0.066					X
5 Fill out maintenance checklist and report deficiencies.	0.022					X

PM8.5-110-1975
BACKFLOW PREVENTION DEVICE, UP TO 4", SPECIAL

(Note: Test frequency may vary depending on local regulations and application.)

	LABOR-HRS	PM FREQUENCY				
		W	M	Q	S	A
Total labor-hours per event		0.000	0.000	0.000	0.333	0.333
Total labor-hours/year by frequency		0.000	0.000	0.000	0.333	0.333
Total labor-hours/year						0.666
1 Test and calibrate check valve operation with test set.	0.191				X	X
2 Bleed air from backflow preventer.	0.047				X	X
3 Inspect for leaks under pressure.	0.007				X	X
4 Clean backflow preventer and surrounding area.	0.066				X	X
5 Fill out maintenance checklist and report deficiencies.	0.022				X	X

PM8.5-110-2975
BACKFLOW PREVENTION DEVICE, OVER 4"
SPECIAL

(Note: Test frequency may vary depending on local regulations and application.)

	LABOR-HRS	PM FREQUENCY				
		W	M	Q	S	A
Total labor-hours per event		0.000	0.000	0.000	0.494	0.494
Total labor-hours/year by frequency		0.000	0.000	0.000	0.494	0.494
Total labor-hours/year						0.988
1 Test and calibrate check valve operation of with test set.	0.334				X	X
2 Bleed air from backflow preventer.	0.065				X	X
3 Inspect for leaks under pressure.	0.007				X	X
4 Clean backflow preventer and surrounding area.	0.066				X	X
5 Fill out maintenance checklist and report deficiencies.	0.022				X	X

PM8.5-170-2950
PUMP, SPLIT-CASE

	LABOR-HRS	PM FREQUENCY				
		W	M	Q	S	A
Total labor-hours per event		0.000	0.000	0.598	0.598	0.598
Total labor-hours/year by frequency		0.000	0.000	1.196	0.598	0.598
Total labor-hours/year						2.392
1 Check for proper operation of pump.	0.022			X	X	X
2 Check for leaks on suction and discharge piping; make minor adjustments as required.	0.029			X	X	X
3 Check that water is dripping properly from packing around shaft.	0.048			X	X	X
4 Check pump and motor operation for excessive vibration, noise and overheating.	0.022			X	X	X
5 Check coupling and alignment of pump and motor; adjust as necessary.	0.260			X	X	X
6 Lubricate pump and motor.	0.099			X	X	X
7 Clean exterior of pump, motor and surrounding area.	0.096			X	X	X
8 Fill out maintenance checklist and report deficiencies.	0.022			X	X	X

PM8.5-320-1950
VALVE, BUTTERFLY, ABOVE 4"

	LABOR-HRS	PM FREQUENCY				
		W	M	Q	S	A
Total labor-hours per event		0.000	0.000	0.000	0.000	0.166
Total labor-hours/year by frequency		0.000	0.000	0.000	0.000	0.166
Total labor-hours/year						0.166
1 Lubricate valve as required.	0.022					X
2 Open and close valve using handle, wrench or hand wheel to check operation.	0.049					X
3 Check for leaks.	0.007					X
4 Clean valve exterior and area around valve.	0.066					X
5 Fill out maintenance checklist and report deficiencies.	0.022					X

PM8.5-340-1950
VALVE, GATE, ABOVE 4"

	LABOR-HRS	PM FREQUENCY				
		W	M	Q	S	A
Total labor-hours per event		0.000	0.000	0.000	0.000	0.159
Total labor-hours/year by frequency		0.000	0.000	0.000	0.000	0.159
Total labor-hours/year						0.159
1 Lubricate valve stem; close and open valve to check operation.	0.049					X
2 Check packing gland for leaks; tighten packing and flange bolts as required.	0.022					X
3 Clean valve exterior and surrounding area.	0.066					X
4 Fill out maintenance checklist and report deficiencies.	0.022					X

PM8.5-350-1950
VALVE, MOTOR OPERATED, ABOVE 4"

	LABOR-HRS	PM FREQUENCY				
		W	M	Q	S	A
Total labor-hours per event		0.000	0.000	0.000	0.501	0.501
Total labor-hours/year by frequency		0.000	0.000	0.000	0.501	0.501
Total labor-hours/year						1.002
1 Lubricate valve actuator stem and valve stem, where possible.	0.091				X	X
2 Check motor and valve for proper operation, including limit switch; adjust as required.	0.022				X	X
3 Check packing gland for leaks; adjust as required.	0.113				X	X
4 Check electrical wiring, connections and contacts; repair as necessary.	0.120				X	X
5 Inspect and lubricate motor gearbox as required.	0.099				X	X
6 Clean valve exterior and surrounding area.	0.034				X	X
7 Fill out maintenance checklist and report deficiencies.	0.022				X	X

PM8.5-355-1950
VALVE, OS&Y, ABOVE 4"

	LABOR-HRS	PM FREQUENCY				
		W	M	Q	S	A
Total labor-hours per event		0.000	0.000	0.000	0.000	0.159
Total labor-hours/year by frequency		0.000	0.000	0.000	0.000	0.159
Total labor-hours/year						0.159
1 Lubricate stem; open and close valve to check operation.	0.049					X
2 Check packing gland for leaks; tighten packing and flange bolts as required.	0.022					X
3 Clean valve exterior and area around valve.	0.066					X
4 Fill out maintenance checklist and report deficiencies.	0.022					X

PM8.5-370-1950
VALVE, SEDIMENT STRAINER, ABOVE 4"

	LABOR-HRS	PM FREQUENCY				
		W	M	Q	S	A
Total labor-hours per event		0.000	0.000	0.000	0.000	0.313
Total labor-hours/year by frequency		0.000	0.000	0.000	0.000	0.313
Total labor-hours/year						0.313
1 Inspect valve for leaks; tighten fittings as necessary.	0.160					X
2 Open valve drain to remove collected sediment.	0.065					X
3 Clean valve exterior and surrounding area.	0.066					X
4 Fill out maintenance checklist and report deficiencies.	0.022					X

PM9.1-150-1950
SWITCHBOARD, ELECTRICAL

	LABOR-HRS	PM FREQUENCY				
		W	M	Q	S	A
Total labor-hours per event		0.000	0.000	0.000	0.000	0.705
Total labor-hours/year by frequency		0.000	0.000	0.000	0.000	0.705
Total labor-hours/year						0.705
1 Check with operating or area personnel for deficiencies.	0.044					X
2 Check indicating lamps for proper operation. If appropriate, replace burned-out lamps.	0.018					X
3 Remove and reinstall cover.	0.196					X
4 Check for discoloration, hot spots, odors and charred insulation.	0.359					X
5 Clean switchboard exterior and surrounding area.	0.066					X
6 Fill out maintenance checklist and report deficiencies.	0.022					X

PM9.1-210-1950
AUTOMATIC TRANSFER SWITCH

	LABOR-HRS	PM FREQUENCY				
		W	M	Q	S	A
Total labor-hours per event		0.000	0.443	0.443	0.443	0.443
Total labor-hours/year by frequency		0.000	3.544	0.886	0.443	0.443
Total labor-hours/year						5.316
1 Check with operating or area personnel for deficiencies.	0.044		X	X	X	X
2 Inspect wiring, wiring connections and fuse blocks for looseness, charring, evidence of short circuiting or overheating and tighten all connections.	0.263		X	X	X	X
3 Inspect general condition of transfer switch and clean exterior and surrounding area.	0.114		X	X	X	X
4 Fill out maintenance checklist and report deficiencies.	0.022		X	X	X	X

PM9.2-110-1950
MOTOR CONTROL CENTER, ELECTRIC

	LABOR-HRS	PM FREQUENCY				
		W	M	Q	S	A
Total labor-hours per event		0.000	0.000	0.000	0.000	0.389
Total labor-hours/year by frequency		0.000	0.000	0.000	0.000	0.389
Total labor-hours/year						0.389
1 Check with operating or area personnel for deficiencies.	0.044					X
2 Check starter lights; replace if required.	0.018					X
3 Check for excessive heat, odors, noise and vibration.	0.239					X
4 Clean motor control center exterior and surrounding area.	0.066					X
5 Fill out maintenance checklist and report deficiencies.	0.022					X

PM9.3-105-2950
GENERATOR, EMERGENCY, DIESEL, OVER 15 KVA

	LABOR-HRS	PM FREQUENCY				
		W	M	Q	S	A
Total labor-hours per event		0.000	1.277	1.277	1.277	2.111
Total labor-hours/year by frequency		0.000	10.216	2.554	1.277	2.111
Total labor-hours/year						16.158
1 Check with operating or area personnel for deficiencies.	0.044		X	X	X	X
2 Check engine oil level; add as required.	0.010		X	X	X	X
3 Change engine oil and oil filter.	0.511					X
4 Check battery charge and electrolyte specific gravity, add water as required; check terminals for corrosion, clean as required.	0.241		X	X	X	X
5 Check belts for wear and proper tension; adjust as necessary.	0.012		X	X	X	X
6 Check that crank case heater is operating.	0.038		X	X	X	X
7 Check engine air filter; change as required.	0.042					X
8 Check wiring, connections, switches, etc.; adjust as required.	0.036		X	X	X	X
9 Check spark plug or injector nozzle condition; service or replace as required.	0.281					X
10 Perform 30 minute generator test run; check for proper operation.	0.650		X	X	X	X
11 Check fuel level with gauge pole; add as required.	0.046		X	X	X	X
12 Wipe dust and dirt from engine and generator.	0.109		X	X	X	X
13 Clean area around generator.	0.066		X	X	X	X
14 Fill out maintenance checklist and report deficiencies.	0.025		X	X	X	X

PM9.3-170-2950
UNINTERRUPTIBLE POWER SYSTEM, 200 TO 800 KVA

	LABOR-HRS	PM FREQUENCY				
		W	M	Q	S	A
Total labor-hours per event		0.000	5.044	9.433	9.433	9.433
Total labor-hours/year by frequency		0.000	40.352	18.866	9.433	9.433
Total labor-hours/year						78.084
1 Check with operating or area personnel for deficiencies.	0.044		X	X	X	X
2 Check electrolyte level of batteries. Add water as required; check terminals for corrosion and clean as required.	3.510		X	X	X	X
3 Check 25% of the batteries for charge and electrolyte specific gravity.	3.107			X	X	X
4 Check batteries for cracks or leaks.	0.585		X	X	X	X
5 Check 25% of the terminal-to-cell connection resistances; rehabilitate connections as required. Add anti-corrosion grease to battery terminals and connections.	0.234			X	X	X
6 Measure and record individual cell and string float voltages.	0.936			X	X	X
7 Check integrity of battery rack.	0.702		X	X	X	X
8 Check battery room temperature and ventilation systems.	0.010		X	X	X	X
9 Replace air filters on UPS modules.	0.036		X	X	X	X
10 Check output voltage and amperages from control panel.	0.007		X	X	X	X
11 Check UPS room temperature and ventilation system.	0.062		X	X	X	X
12 Notify proper personnel and test UPS fault alarm system.	0.112			X	X	X
13 Clean around batteries and UPS modules.	0.066		X	X	X	X
14 Fill out maintenance checklist and report deficiencies.	0.022		X	X	X	X

APPENDIX/INDEX

- *Return-on-Investment Models*
- *How Does Your PM Program Rate?*
- *Integrating CMMS*
- *Resources*
- *Index*

RETURN-ON-INVESTMENT MODELS

A PM Return-on-Investment model that relates to short-term resources with long-term payback savings can only be approximated. In the analysis that follows, cash-flow scenarios have been developed to estimate the cost of PM, significant repairs, and minor collateral damage to associated equipment. Upgrades for two typical types of equipment that might be found in any building have also been analyzed. For illustrative purposes, the time value of money is not a part of this analysis; all dollars are shown as constant.

Equipment Type A represents a 10-ton package air conditioner that costs $15,588, has a 15-year life span with PM performed, and 10 years without PM. The cost to perform PM is $164 per annum.

Equipment Type B is a 25-HP hot water circulating pump that costs $4,351, has a 20-year life span with PM performed, and 15 years without PM. The cost to perform the PM is $53 per annum.

The Cash-Flow Tabulation of Equipment Type A indicates that the equipment with PM performed would require two replacements during the period that the same equipment without PM would require three replacements. An overall savings of $35,542, or 44.2%, in present-day money, would result by performing PM. Removal of the collateral damage expenses ($3,500) and additional upgrade expenses ($2,500) from consideration would result in saving $32,042, or 39.8%, by performing PM. Refer to Figure A.1 for the Cash-Flow Tabulation Worksheet for Equipment Type A.

The Cash-Flow Tabulation of Equipment Type B indicates that the equipment with PM performed would require three replacements during the period that the same equipment without PM performed would require four replacements. An overall savings of $24,247, or

44.5%, in present-day money, would result by performing PM. Removal of the collateral damage expenses ($5,700) from consideration would result in saving $18,546, or 34.0%, by performing PM. Refer to Figure A.2 for the Cash-Flow Tabulation Worksheet for Equipment Type B.

Using the above assumptions, and extrapolating equipment for the buildings on a normal campus, considerable long-term savings would result due to the implementation of a PM program. Additionally, basic engineering and management practice would dictate that any unscheduled equipment failure should be avoided if at all possible due to the potential costs of significant collateral damage due to service interruption.

Cash-Flow Tabulation for Equipment Type A
Used to select one of two alternatives based upon incremental rate of return

Package Air Conditioning Unit - free standing, water cooled, 10 ton

| | Model With Preventive Maintenance | | | | | Model Without Preventive Maintenance | | | | | | | |
Equipment Cost	Cost of Equipment	Annual PM Cost	Significant Repairs	Equipment Upgrades	Equipment Age	Equipment Cost	Cost of Equipment	Significant Repairs	Collateral Damage	Equipment Upgrades	PM Cash Flow YES	PM Cash Flow NO	Net Cash Flow
$15,588						$15,588							
	$1,039	$164			1		$1,559				$1,203	$1,559	$356
	$1,039	$164			2		$1,559				$1,203	$1,559	$356
	$1,039	$164			3		$1,559	$5,421			$1,203	$6,980	$5,777
	$1,039	$164			4		$1,559				$1,203	$1,559	$356
	$1,039	$164	$626		5		$1,559	$2,550	$1,000		$1,829	$5,109	$3,280
	$1,039	$164			6		$1,559				$1,203	$1,559	$356
	$1,039	$164			7		$1,559				$1,203	$1,559	$356
	$1,039	$164			8		$1,559	$626			$1,203	$2,185	$982
	$1,039	$164			9		$1,559				$1,203	$1,559	$356
	$1,039	$164	$2,550		10	$15,588	$1,559				$3,753	$1,559	-$2,194
	$1,039	$164			11		$1,559				$1,203	$1,559	$356
	$1,039	$164			12		$1,559	$2,548			$1,203	$4,107	$2,904
	$1,039	$164		$2,500	13		$1,559			$2,500	$3,703	$4,059	$356
	$1,039	$164			14		$1,559	$5,421			$1,203	$6,980	$5,777
$15,588	$1,039	$164			15		$1,559				$1,203	$1,559	$356
	$1,039	$164			16		$1,559				$1,203	$1,559	$356
	$1,039	$164			17		$1,559				$1,203	$1,559	$356
	$1,039	$164			18		$1,559	$2,550	$1,750		$1,203	$5,859	$4,656
	$1,039	$164			19		$1,559				$1,203	$1,559	$356
	$1,039	$164	$626		20	$15,588	$1,559				$1,829	$1,559	-$270
	$1,039	$164			21		$1,559				$1,203	$1,559	$356
	$1,039	$164			22		$1,559	$626			$1,203	$2,185	$982
	$1,039	$164			23		$1,559				$1,203	$1,559	$356
	$1,039	$164			24		$1,559				$1,203	$1,559	$356
	$1,039	$164	$2,550		25		$1,559	$5,421			$3,753	$6,980	$3,227
	$1,039	$164			26		$1,559				$1,203	$1,559	$356
	$1,039	$164			27		$1,559				$1,203	$1,559	$356
	$1,039	$164			28		$1,559	$2,550	$750		$1,203	$4,859	$3,656
	$1,039	$164			29		$1,559				$1,203	$1,559	$356
$15,588	$1,039	$164			30	$15,588	$1,559				$1,203	$1,559	$356
	$31,170	$4,920	$6,353	$2,500			$46,770	$27,715	$3,500	$2,500			

Totals | $44,943 | $80,485 | $35,542

Notes:
1. Dollars are in present worth dollars, not time valued.
2. The model without PM requires replacement in year 15 ($15,588/15 years = $1,039/year expenditure).
3. The model with PM requires replacement in year 10 ($15,588/10 years = $1,559/year expenditure).

FIGURE A.1

Cash-Flow Tabulation for Equipment Type B

Used to select one of two alternatives based upon incremental rate of return

Centrifugal Circulating Pump - base mount, 25 HP

	Model With Preventive Maintenance						Model Without Preventive Maintenance						
Age	Equipment Cost	Cost of Equipment	Annual PM Cost	Significant Repairs	Equipment Upgrades	Equipment Cost	Cost of Equipment	Significant Repairs	Collateral Damage	Equipment Upgrades	PM Cash Flow YES	PM Cash Flow NO	Net Cash Flow
0	$4,351	$218	$53			$4,351	$290						
1		$218	$53				$290				$271	$290	$19
2		$218	$53				$290	$198			$271	$488	$217
3		$218	$53				$290				$271	$290	$19
4		$218	$53				$290				$271	$290	$19
5		$218	$53				$290	$442			$271	$732	$461
6		$218	$53				$290				$271	$290	$19
7		$218	$53	$2,304			$290	$2,304	$750		$2,575	$3,344	$769
8		$218	$53				$290				$271	$290	$19
9		$218	$53				$290	$198			$271	$488	$217
10		$218	$53				$290				$271	$290	$19
11		$218	$53	$198			$290				$469	$290	-$179
12		$218	$53				$290	$2,734	$1,500		$271	$4,524	$4,253
13		$218	$53	$442			$290				$713	$290	-$423
14		$218	$53				$290	$442			$271	$732	$461
15		$218	$53			$4,351	$290				$271	$290	$19
16		$218	$53				$290				$271	$290	$19
17		$218	$53				$290	$198	$450		$271	$938	$667
18		$218	$53	$198			$290				$469	$290	-$179
19		$218	$53				$290				$271	$290	$19
20	$4,351	$218	$53				$290	$442			$271	$732	$461
21		$218	$53				$290				$271	$290	$19
22		$218	$53				$290	$2,304	$1,250		$271	$3,844	$3,573
23		$218	$53				$290				$271	$290	$19
24		$218	$53				$290	$198			$271	$488	$217
25		$218	$53				$290				$271	$290	$19
26		$218	$53				$290				$271	$290	$19
27		$218	$53	$2,304			$290	$2,734	$1,750		$2,575	$4,774	$2,199
28		$218	$53				$290				$271	$290	$19
29		$218	$53				$290	$442			$271	$732	$461
30		$218	$53			$4,351	$290				$271	$290	$19
31		$218	$53				$290				$271	$290	$19
32		$218	$53	$198			$290	$198	$200		$469	$688	$219
33		$218	$53				$290				$271	$290	$19
34		$218	$53	$2,734			$290				$3,005	$290	-$2,715
35		$218	$53				$290	$442			$271	$732	$461
36		$218	$53				$290				$271	$290	$19
37		$218	$53				$290	$2,304	$1,000		$271	$3,594	$3,323
38		$218	$53	$198			$290				$469	$290	-$179
39		$218	$53				$290	$198			$271	$488	$217
40	$4,351	$218	$53				$290				$271	$290	$19
41		$218	$53				$290				$271	$290	$19
42		$218	$53				$290	$2,734	$1,500		$271	$4,524	$4,253
43		$218	$53				$290				$271	$290	$19
44		$218	$53				$290	$442			$271	$732	$461
45		$218	$53			$4,351	$290				$271	$290	$19
46		$218	$53				$290				$271	$290	$19
47		$218	$53	$2,304			$290	$198	$450		$2,575	$938	-$1,637
48		$218	$53				$290				$271	$290	$19
49		$218	$53				$290				$271	$290	$19
50		$218	$53				$290	$442			$271	$732	$461
51		$218	$53	$198			$290				$469	$290	-$179
52		$218	$53				$290	$2,304	$1,250		$271	$3,844	$3,573
53		$218	$53	$2,734			$290				$3,005	$290	-$2,715
54		$218	$53				$290	$198			$271	$488	$217
55		$218	$53				$290				$271	$290	$19
56		$218	$53				$290				$271	$290	$19
57		$218	$53				$290	$2,734	$1,750		$271	$4,774	$4,503
58		$218	$53	$198			$290				$469	$290	-$179
59		$218	$53				$290	$442			$271	$732	$461
60	$4,351	$218	$53			$4,351	$290				$271	$290	$19
		$13,080	$3,180	$5,445			$17,400	$12,434	$5,700				

Totals	$30,267	$54,514	$24,247

Notes:

1. Dollars are in present worth dollars, not time valued.
2. The model without PM requires replacement in year 20 ($4,351/20 years = $218/year expenditure).
3. The model with PM requires replacement in year 15 ($4,351/15 years = $290/year expenditure).

FIGURE A.2

HOW DOES YOUR PM PROGRAM RATE?

The following questionnaire, derived from *The Maintenance Management Audit*, published by R.S. Means Company, was designed to allow facilities managers to evaluate their PM program. To use the checklist, place a checkmark in the appropriate "Yes" or "No" box for each of the following questions. When you have finished, total the number of "Yes" answers, and refer to the rating system at the end. Thirteen "Yes" answers means that the PM program, as in place, is excellent. Less than five "Yes" answers indicates that the PM program could be stronger. This checklist will help you identify the areas for improvement.

YES NO

Procedures Established:

☐ ☐ Have all facilities-related equipment items appropriate to PM been identified?

☐ ☐ Have PM standards been prepared for each item in the program?

☐ ☐ Do they include checkpoints, frequency of inspection, and time required to perform PM?

Work Orders Issued and Personnel Assigned:

☐ ☐ Are work orders prepared and issued for authorized PM work?

☐ ☐ Do they include PM checklists and indicate the allotted times to perform PM for each piece of equipment on the work order?

☐ ☐ Are personnel qualified and trained to perform PM?

☐ ☐ Are definite limits set and adhered to for the amount of time allotted to the work orders?

☐ ☐ Are provisions made for recording the results of PM and comments about the equipment?

☐ ☐ Have specific responsibilities for operator-performed PM been documented within the standard operating procedures?

☐ ☐ Have annual PM plans and weekly PM schedules been established?

☐ ☐ Are they consistent with the shop-hours available to accomplish this work?

Preventive Maintenance Work Performance:

☐ ☐ Is PM work being accomplished within 10% of the PM schedule?

☐ ☐ Is the PM schedule performance being documented and reviewed by management?

Equipment Records:

☐ ☐ Are the equipment records maintained and periodically reviewed for general condition, cost trends, downtime, replacement requirements, etc.?

☐ ☐ Do these records automatically flag problem items?

Use the following chart to find your program index rating. Total all of the "Yes" answers.

Number of YES Answers	Your PM Program Rating
Over 13	Excellent
8 to 12	Good
5 to 7	Fair
Under 5	Poor

INTEGRATING CMMS

Many organizations attempt to implement their PM program with the purchase of a Computerized Maintenance Management System (CMMS). If at all possible, basic PM parameters should be achieved *before* the software system takes over. Specifically, the facility manager must decide which facilities, pieces of equipment, checkpoints, and frequencies will be included.

After a decision to acquire a CMMS system is made, the data from the PM program can be incorporated during the CMMS implementation phase. The vehicle used to transfer this data is normally aided by a routine supplied by the CMMS vendor.

CMMS Acquisition

While the purchase of a CMMS system is relatively simple, the actual selection requires careful consideration. Many CMMS systems are never completely implemented for many reasons. The following is a sample list of features that should be included—and fully implemented—in a CMMS.

- Import/export capabilities
- Ability to handle comprehensive library of checklists (capable of being edited)
- Inventory tracking and system maintenance capabilities
- PM work schedules and work orders development capabilities
- Ability to capture historical data and generate trends
- Ability to produce useful summary reports
- User friendly

Typically, an understanding of the resources and business decisions necessary to implement are understated, and a detailed schedule and plan is not developed. After the basic modules such as service calls are operational, the emphasis and momentum decreases. The following acquisition milestones will help facility managers, staff, customers, and management understand the total impact of the CMMS/PM issue.

Focus Groups

The CMMS system must be either developed or purchased around the needs of the users. A good way to start a discussion of CMMS requirements is the use of focus groups. These can start on a one-on-one basis and evolve to group meetings. Conversely, they can evolve from group to one-on-one sessions. However, the essential part of this process is that the CMMS needs of the various users are recognized.

Documentation of Requirements

The next step is to organize the facility's CMMS needs in writing. The requirements documentation can take the form of:

- Memo of understanding
- White paper
- Technical report of specified requirements

Whatever form of documentation, the essential part of the process is for key members of focus groups to have an opportunity to see and comment on their input and the input of others. There may be several interactions to this process, but the result will stand as the baseline specification for the CMMS acquisition. A requirements document would be developed to define the specific requirements that are to be included in the CMMS. This is the most important phase when starting the search for a CMMS.

RFP Development

A request for price (RFP) should be developed that contains a detailed list of the requirements that the university is looking for in a CMMS. Unlike the purchase of a product, such as a standard office assistant or program, the CMMS acquisition will tend to look more like the purchase of a counseling services RFP. In essence, a scope will be written describing what the organization wants, and the provider will define how the need is to be covered. The university should expect that no two proposals will be exactly the same technically.

CMMS Selection

The selection process should include a demonstration of the system and the functionality that responds to each requirement in the RFP. The cost structure, especially for implementation, should be clearly defined by the vendor. It is important to note that most successful CMMS implementation costs much more than the actual licensing costs, whether it is accomplished by in-house staff or as part of the vendor's service.

RESOURCES

The following organizations can be contacted for a variety of information applicable to the maintenance of higher education facilities, including useful articles, products, and links to other resources.

American Public Works Association (APWA)
2345 Grand Blvd.
Suite 500
Kansas City, MO 64108
816-472-6100
http://www.pubworks.org

American School and University
9800 Metcalf Street
Overland Park, KS 66212
913-341-1300
http://www.asumag.com

Association for Facilities Engineering (AFE)
8081 Corporate Park Drive
Suite 305
Cincinnati, OH 45242
513-489-2473
http://www.afe.org

Association of College & University Housing Officers International (ACUHO-I)
941 Chatham Lane
Suite 318
Columbus, OH 43221-2416
614-292-0099
http://www.acuho-i.org

Association of Higher Education Facilities Officers (APPA)
1643 Prince Street
Alexandria, VA 22314
703-684-1446
http://www.appa.org

Building Owners and Managers Association (BOMA)
1201 New York Avenue, NW
Suite 300
Washington, DC 20005
202-408-2662
http://www.boma.org

Council of Educational Facility Planners, International (CEFPI)
9180 E. Desert Cove
Suite 104
Scottsdale, AZ 85258
480-391-0840
http://www.cefpi.org

Council of Higher Education Management Association (CHEMA)
2501 M Street NW
Suite 400
Washington, DC 20037
202-861-2577
http://www.chemanet.org

FacilitiesNet
http://www.facilitiesnet.com

facilitymanagement.com
http://www.facilitymanagement.com

This Website is the on-line site of *American School & Hospital Magazine.*

FMLink
FMLink Group, LLC
P.O. Box 59557
Potomac, MD 20859
http://www.fmlink.com

Group C Communications, Inc.
121 Monmouth Street
Red Bank, NJ 07701

International City/County Management Association (ICMA)
777 N. Capitol Street NE
Suite 500
Washington, DC 20002
202-289-4262
http://www.icma.org

International Facility Management Association (IFMA)
1 E. Greenway Plaza
Suite 1100
Houston, TX 77046
713-623-4362
http://www.ifma.org

International Maintenance Institute (IMI)
P.O. Box 751896
Houston, TX 77275
281-481-0869
http://www.imionline.org

National Association of College & University Business Officers (NACUBO)
2501 M Street NW
Suite 400
Washington, DC 20037
202-861-2500
http://www.nacubo.org

National Association of State Facilities Administrators (NASFA)
2760 Research Park Dr.
P.O. Box 11910
Lexington, KY 40578-1910
859-244-8181
http://www.nasfa.net

National Clearinghouse for Educational Facilities (NCEF)
1090 Vermont Avenue, NW
Suite 700
Washington, DC 20005
888-552-0624
http://www.edfacilities.org

National Education Association (NEA)
1201 16th Street NW
Washington, DC 20036
202-833-4000
http://www.nea.org

Society of College and University Planners (SCUP)
311 Maynard Street
Ann Arbor, MI 48104
734-998-7832
http://www.scup.org

INDEX

NOTES

NOTES